MathFlare

Name: _________________________

Class: ___________

Teacher: _________________________

Introduction

As parents and educators, we recognize the pivotal role mathematics plays in shaping a child's academic journey and future success. Yet, the path to mathematical proficiency can often seem daunting, fraught with challenges and complexities. That's where the transformative power of MathFlare Workbooks shine through, illuminating the way forward with clarity, precision, and purpose.

Introducing MathFlare Workbooks – a beacon of guidance, a testament to excellence, and a catalyst for achievement. Crafted with meticulous care and expertise, MathFlare Workbooks stand as paragons of educational excellence, designed to nurture young minds, ignite a passion for learning, and develop a deep-rooted understanding of mathematical concepts.

Picture this: your child eagerly delves into the pages of Mathflare Workbook, greeted by a step-by-step guide illuminated with vivid examples that demystify complex mathematical concepts. With each turn of the page, they embark on a journey of discovery, encountering thoughtfully curated practice questions that reinforce learning and hone problem-solving skills. And when they unveil the answers to those very questions, a sense of accomplishment blossoms within them – a tangible reward for their hard work and dedication.

But MathFlare Workbooks are more than just tools for learning; they are pathways to comprehension, fostering a deep-seated understanding of mathematical concepts through a sequential, logical flow. From fundamental principles to advanced problem-solving strategies, every chapter builds upon the last, ensuring a robust foundation upon which future knowledge can be constructed.

As parents, we yearn for nothing more than to see our children thrive, to witness the spark of inspiration ignited within them as they conquer academic challenges with confidence and poise. MathFlare Workbooks serve as partners in this noble endeavor, offering not just practice questions, but the keys to unlocking a world of opportunity.

And for teachers, MathFlare Workbooks stand as invaluable allies in the quest to cultivate mathematical proficiency in the classroom. With answers readily available, instructors can focus on guiding and nurturing their students, confident in the knowledge that MathFlare Workbooks provide a solid framework upon which to build.

In the pages of MathFlare Workbooks, we find not just the promise of academic excellence, but the seeds of a brighter tomorrow. So let us embrace the power of mathematics, let us champion the journey of learning, and let us pave the way for a generation of young minds poised to shape the world. With MathFlare Workbooks as our guide, the possibilities are infinite, and the future, bright.

Table of Contents

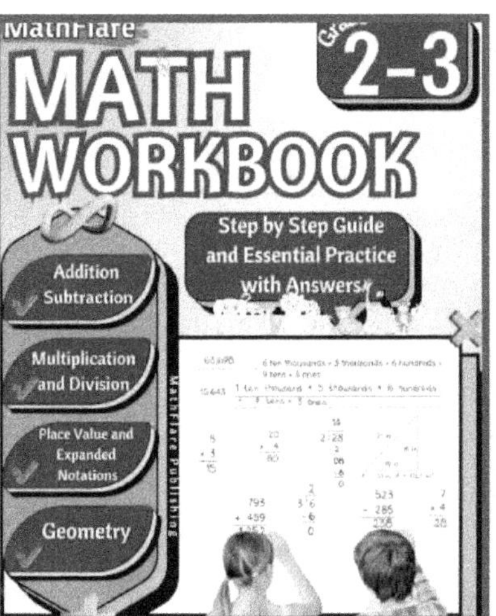

MathFlare
Grade 5
MATH WORKBOOK
Step by Step Guide and Essential Practice with Answers
Multiplication Division
Place Value and Expanded Notations
Fractions and Geometry
Unit Conversion
MathFlare Publishing

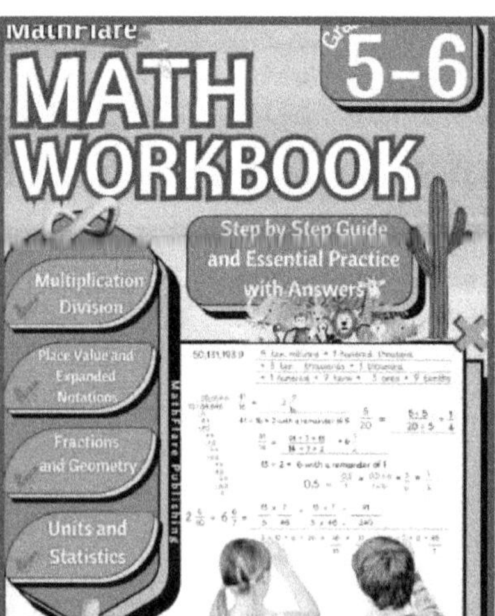
MathFlare
Grade 5-6
MATH WORKBOOK
Step by Step Guide and Essential Practice with Answers
Multiplication Division
Place Value and Expanded Notations
Fractions and Geometry
Units and Statistics
MathFlare Publishing

MathFlare
Grade 6
MATH WORKBOOK
Step by Step Guide and Essential Practice with Answers
Integers and Statistics
Arithmetic and Pre-Algebra
Fractions and Geometry
Ratio and Percentage
MathFlare Publishing

MathFlare
Grade 6-7
MATH WORKBOOK
Step by Step Guide and Essential Practice with Answers
Arithmetic and Pre-Algebra
Ratio, Percent Proportion
Geometry
Statistics
MathFlare Publishing

MathFlare
Grade 7
MATH WORKBOOK
Step by Step Guide and Essential Practice with Answers
Pre-Algebra
Ratio, Percent Proportion
Geometry
Statistics
MathFlare Publishing

MathFlare
Grade 7-8
MATH WORKBOOK
Step by Step Guide and Essential Practice with Answers
Pre-Algebra
Ratio, Percent Proportion
Geometry and Cartesian Plane
Statistics
MathFlare Publishing

MathFlare
Grade 8-9
MATH WORKBOOK
Step by Step Guide and Essential Practice with Answers
Pre-Algebra
Ratio, Proportion and Percentage
Linear Equations
Geometry and Cartesian Plane
MathFlare Publishing

MathFlare
Grade 8
MATH WORKBOOK
Step by Step Guide and Essential Practice with Answers
Pre-Algebra
Percentage
Linear Equations
Geometry
MathFlare Publishing

Linear Equation

A linear equation is an algebraic equation that represents a straight line when graphed on a coordinate plane. It consists of variables raised to the power of 1 (i.e., no exponents higher than 1) and constant coefficients.

The general form of a linear equation in one variable x is:

$$ax + b = 0$$

Where a and b are constants, and x is the variable.

Let's solve the linear equation:

$$-2x + 9 = 5$$

- **Isolate the variable term:** We want to isolate the term containing x on one side of the equation. To do this, we'll move the constant term to the other side. Subtract 9 from both sides:

$$-2x + 9 - 9 = 5 - 9$$

$$-2x = -4$$

- **Divide by the coefficient of the variable:** To solve for x, divide both sides by the coefficient of x, which is -2:

$$\frac{-2x}{-2} = \frac{-4}{-2}$$

$$x = 2$$

<u>Slop from Two Points</u>

The slope between two points on a Cartesian coordinate system is a measure of the steepness of the line connecting those points. It's calculated by finding the change in the y-coordinates divided by the change in the x-coordinates.

- The coordinates of the first point as $(x_1, y_1) = (2, -30)$.

- The coordinates of the second point as $(x_2, y_2) = (-5, 40)$.

The formula to calculate the slope (m) between two points:

$$\frac{y2 - y1}{x2 - x1}$$

$$= \frac{40 - (-30)}{-5 - 2} = \frac{70}{-7}$$

$$\text{Slope} = -10$$

<u>Plot Lines</u>

To plot the lines using the given points, we'll first locate each point on the coordinate plane, and then connect the points to form the lines. Let's plot each line one by one:

A = (-6, -3)	B = (0, 3)
C = (-4, -1)	D = (1, 4)
E = (4, 7)	F = (2, 5)

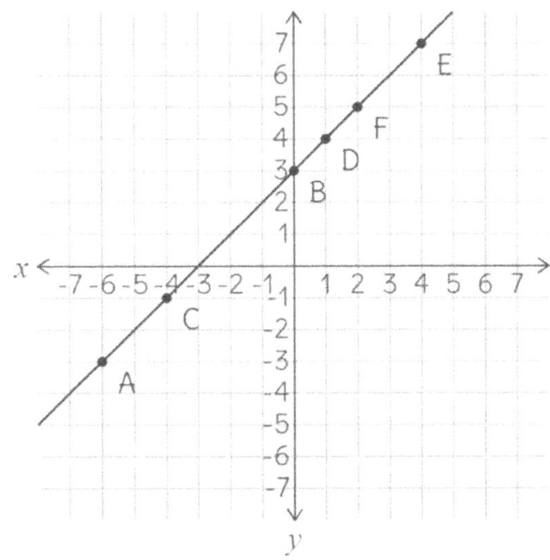

Graphing Linear Equation

Graphing a linear equation involves plotting the points that satisfy the equation on a coordinate plane and connecting them to form a straight line. Linear equations are equations of the form $y = mx + b$, where m represents the slope of the line, and b represents the y-intercept, the point where the line intersects the y-axis.

To graph a linear equation:

1. Identify the slope (m) and y-intercept (b) from the equation.

2. Plot the y-intercept $(0, b)$) as a point on the y-axis.

3. Use the slope to find additional points on the line. The slope represents the change in y for every unit change in x.

4. Connect the points to form a straight line.

For example, to graph the equation:

$$y = \frac{9}{4} x - 8$$

1. **Identify the slope and y-intercept:** The slope is $\frac{9}{4}$, and the y-intercept is −8.

2. **Plot the y-intercept:** Plot the point (0,−8).

3. **Use the slope to plot additional points:** the slop is $\frac{9}{4}$ to find another point. we will move up 9 units and 4 units to the right from the y-intercept to find another point.

4. **Draw the line:** Once we have at least two points, we can draw a straight line.

We can continue this process to plot more points and extend the line further if needed.

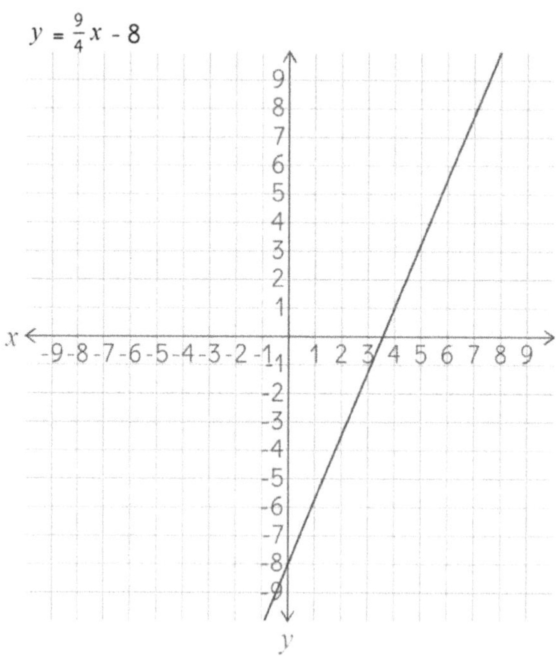

System of Equations

A system of equations is a collection of two or more equations involving the same set of variables. The solution to a system of equations is the set of values for the variables that satisfy all the equations simultaneously.

Solving by Elimination:

To solve a system of equations by elimination, we manipulate the equations to eliminate one of the variables.

Given the system:

$$4x + 5y = 6$$

$$10x + 6y = 8$$

Step 1: Multiply each equation by a constant such that the coefficients of one of the variables become equal or multiples of each other.

Let's try to eliminate the variable x.

- Multiply the first equation by 5 and the second equation by -2:

$$20x + 25y = 30$$

$$-20x - 12y = -16$$

Step 2: Add the two equations together to eliminate the variable x.

$$(20x - 20x) + (25y - 12y) = 30 - 16$$

$$13y = 14$$

$$y = \frac{14}{13} = 1.077$$

Step 3: Solve for y:

Step 4: Substitute the value of y into one of the original equations to solve for x. Let's use the first equation:

$$4x + 5\left(\frac{14}{13}\right) = 6$$

$$4x + \frac{70}{13} = 6$$

$$4x = 6 - \frac{70}{13}$$

$$4x = \frac{78 - 70}{13}$$

$$4x = \frac{8}{13}$$

$$X = \frac{2}{13} = 0.154$$

the solution to the system of equations is x =0.154 and y = 1.077.

Understanding Linear Functions

1. f(x) = -5x + -8, find f(3)

2. f(x) = 3x + 2, find f(-9)

3. f(x) = -4x + -2, find f(4)

4. f(x) = 3x + -3, find f(-5)

5. f(x) = -5x + 4, find f(10)

6. f(x) = -1x + 4, find f(-10)

7. f(x) = 2x + 5, find f(-7)

8. f(x) = -1x + 7, find f(-10)

9. f(x) = 3x + -1, find f(-3)

10. f(x) = 5x + 4, find f(-5)

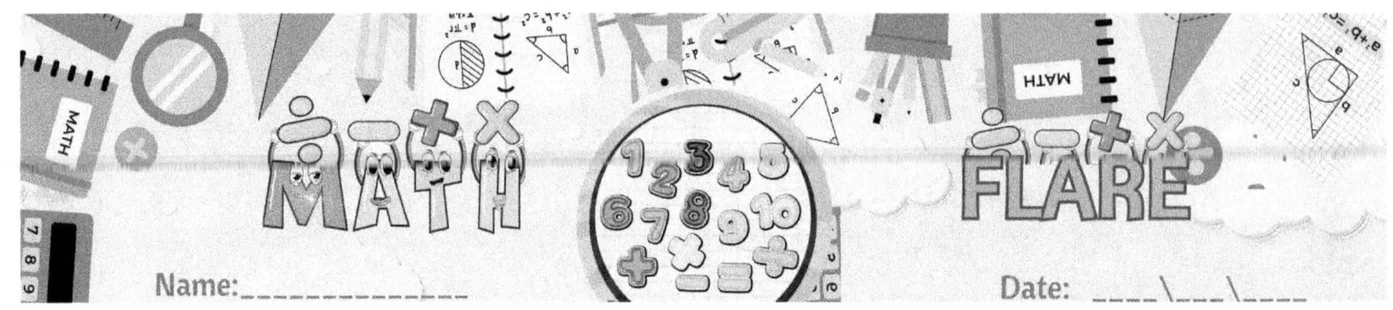

Name:_________________   Date: _______________

11. f(x) = 2x + 8, find f(-2)

16. f(x) = 2x + 8, find f(8)

12. f(x) = 4x + -4, find f(-5)

17. f(x) = 1x + 1, find f(-4)

13. f(x) = 5x + 3, find f(-10)

18. f(x) = -5x + -2, find f(-8)

14. f(x) = -4x + 3, find f(2)

19. f(x) = 4x + -9, find f(-5)

15. f(x) = 1x + 3, find f(7)

20. f(x) = -3x + -6, find f(-2)

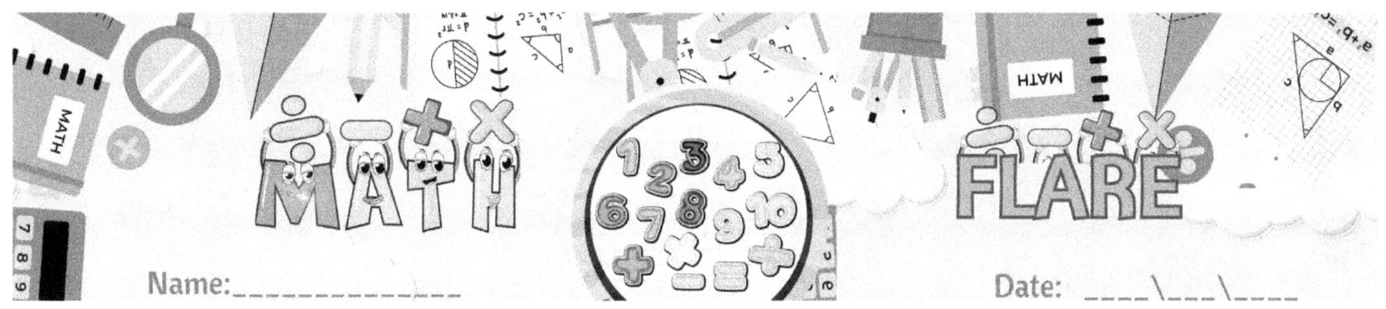

21. f(x) = -1x + 5, find f(-7)

26. f(x) = -1x + -2, find f(3)

22. f(x) = -3x + -8, find f(4)

27. f(x) = -3x + 3, find f(-1)

23. f(x) = -1x + 2, find f(-8)

28. f(x) = -3x + -7, find f(1)

24. f(x) = -4x + -10, find f(7)

29. f(x) = 5x + -3, find f(2)

25. f(x) = 0x + 1, find f(9)

30. f(x) = 3x + 7, find f(-6)

31. $f(x) = -4x + 1$, find $f(3)$

36. $f(x) = -3x + -1$, find $f(10)$

32. $f(x) = -3x + -3$, find $f(-6)$

37. $f(x) = 1x + 3$, find $f(-1)$

33. $f(x) = -5x + -8$, find $f(-5)$

38. $f(x) = -3x + -3$, find $f(1)$

34. $f(x) = 0x + -8$, find $f(-6)$

39. $f(x) = -4x + 1$, find $f(-5)$

35. $f(x) = 5x + 9$, find $f(5)$

40. $f(x) = 0x + 1$, find $f(9)$

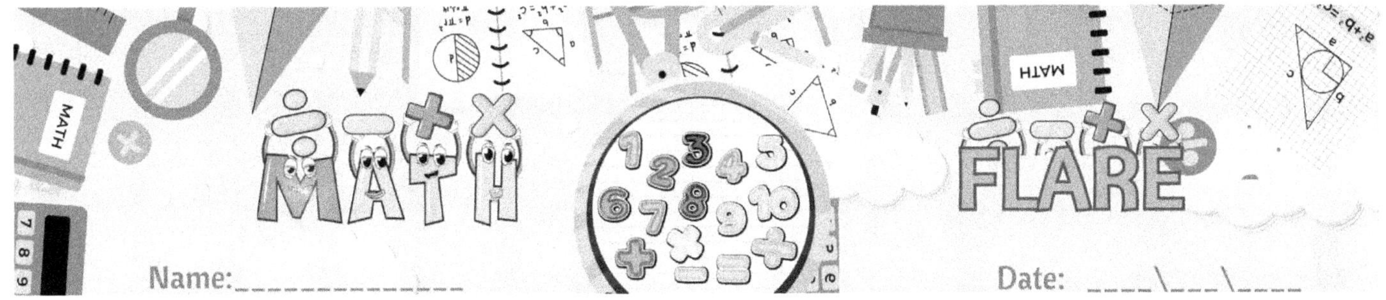

41. f(x) = 3x + -2, find f(-3)

42. f(x) = 0x + 9, find f(-3)

43. f(x) = 1x + 6, find f(0)

44. f(x) = 5x + 7, find f(-9)

45. f(x) = 2x + 6, find f(3)

46. f(x) = 4x + -8, find f(4)

47. f(x) = 0x + 1, find f(3)

48. f(x) = -2x + 5, find f(-8)

49. f(x) = -1x + -8, find f(-7)

50. f(x) = -5x + 8, find f(-5

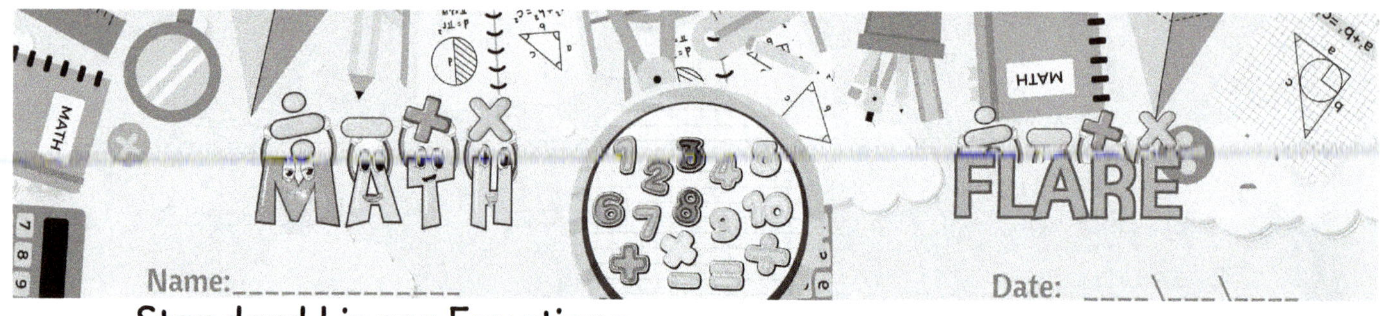

Name:________________ Date: ____________

Standard Linear Equations

1. $-1x + 1 = -2$

2. $6x + -4 = -40$

3. $6x + 4 = 58$

4. $1x + 10 = 2$

5. $-4x + -9 = -41$

6. $9x + -4 = -76$

7. $1x + -5 = -9$

8. $2x + -6 = -6$

9. $-10x + 10 = 20$

10. $-1x + 5 = 10$

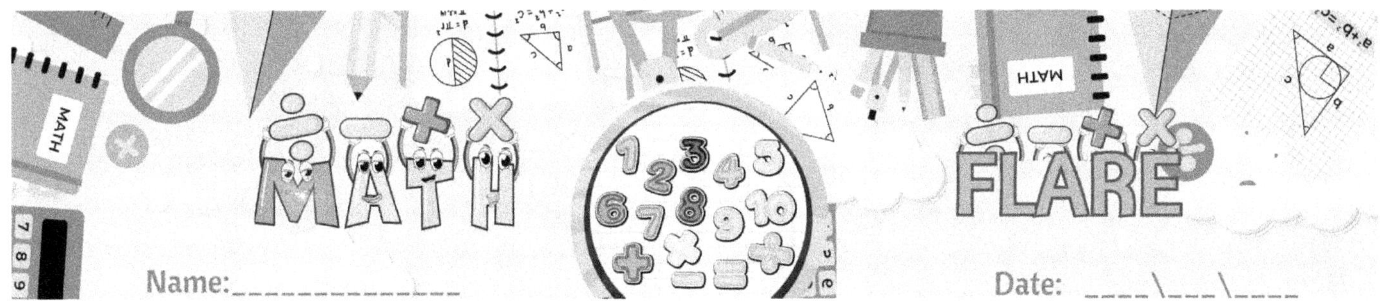

11. $7x + 3 = -53$

16. $6x + 3 = 21$

12. $10x + 2 = 42$

17. $10x + -5 = 55$

13. $10x + 2 = -28$

18. $8x + -8 = -64$

14. $-7x + -8 = -57$

19. $5x + 1 = 31$

15. $4x + -4 = -40$

20. $7x + -10 = 46$

21. $-10x + -2 = -32$

22. $5x + 10 = 5$

23. $4x + 4 = -12$

24. $-4x + 6 = 6$

25. $6x + 4 = -56$

26. $-7x + 9 = 23$

27. $1x + 5 = 6$

28. $-7x + 7 = -63$

29. $-10x + -7 = 33$

30. $-1x + 5 = -1$

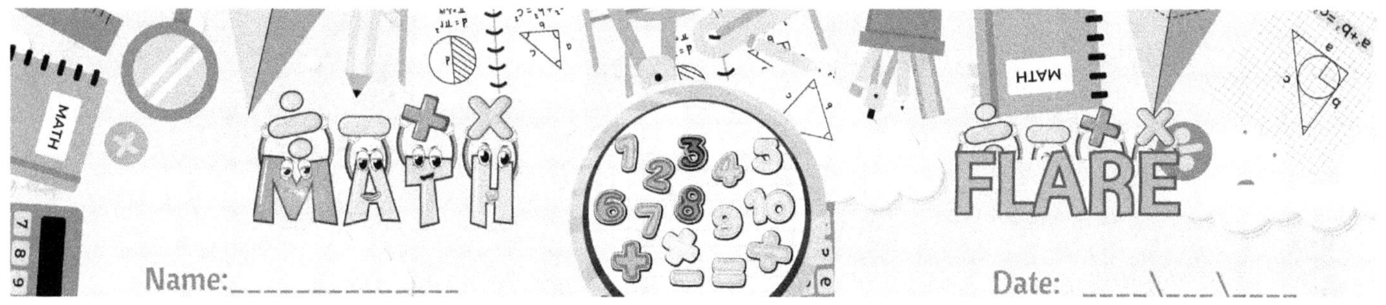

31. $-7x + 5 = -37$

36. $-6x + -10 = -22$

32. $-3x + -7 = -22$

37. $-2x + -4 = 8$

33. $9x + -2 = -74$

38. $7x + -1 = -8$

34. $10x + 3 = 33$

39. $9x + -8 = -8$

35. $10x + -7 = -77$

40. $-5x + 3 = -17$

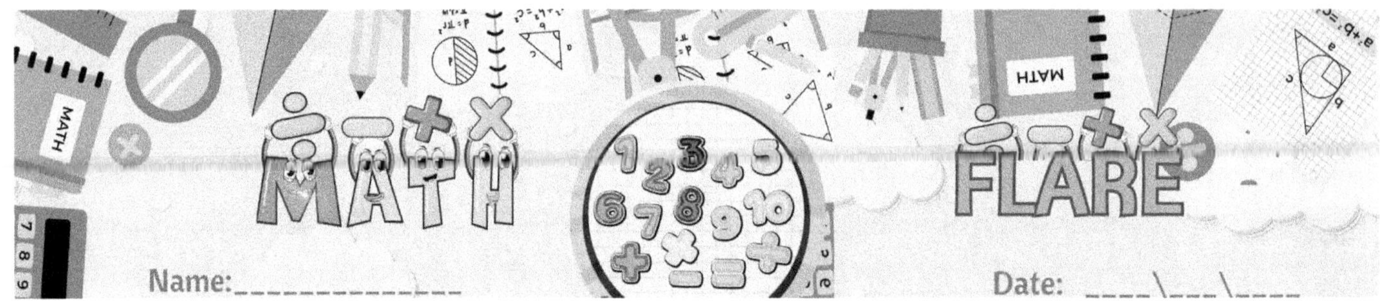

41. $-10x + 1 = 1$

42. $-5x + 4 = 19$

43. $7x + 9 = -40$

44. $-3x + -9 = 15$

45. $-8x + 8 = 24$

46. $2x + -4 = -24$

47. $-8x + 5 = -51$

48. $6x + 2 = -4$

49. $1x + -10 = -16$

50. $-5x + -7 = -2$

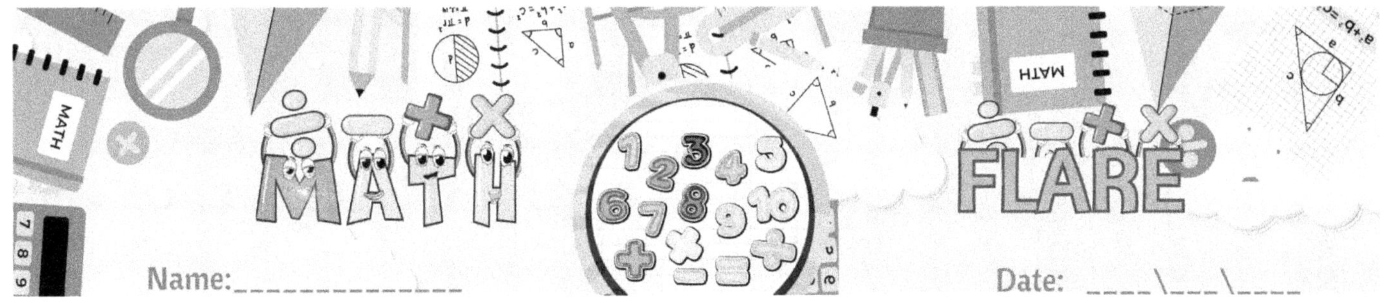

51. $2x + 5 = 7$

52. $-4x + 5 = -19$

53. $5x + 0 = -15$

54. $2x + -1 = 17$

55. $8x + 6 = 54$

56. $3x + 8 = -22$

57. $-2x + 5 = 13$

58. $1x + -9 = -5$

59. $-5x + 10 = 40$

60. $5x + -9 = 1$

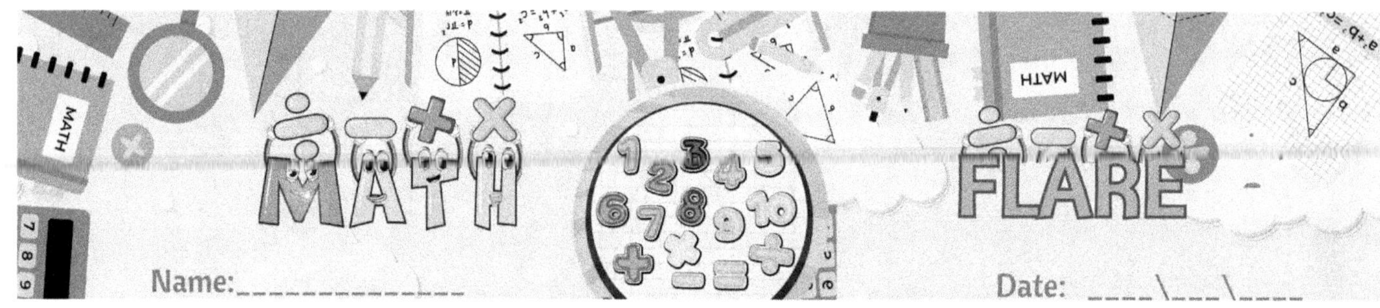

61. -5x + 8 = 28

66. 3x + 9 = -18

62. -7x + -6 = 43

67. -2x + -7 = -17

63. -10x + -7 = 93

68. -8x + -10 = -34

64. 6x + -5 = -11

69. -1x + 0 = 4

65. 1x + 4 = 8

70. 10x + -10 = 30

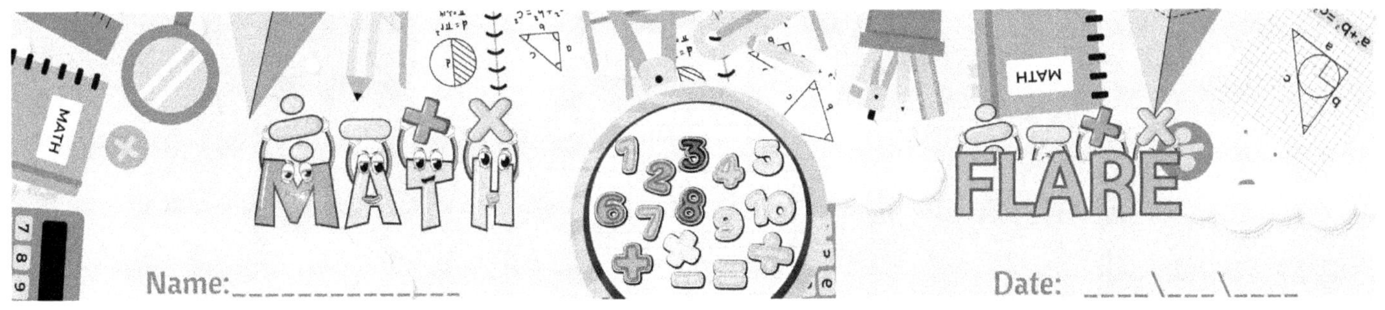

71. $-4x + -8 = 0$

76. $-3x + 2 = -28$

72. $4x + 5 = -19$

77. $3x + -5 = 7$

73. $-7x + -2 = 47$

78. $-3x + 10 = -5$

74. $-9x + -4 = 23$

79. $-5x + 4 = 29$

75. $7x + -2 = 54$

80. $-10x + -2 = 88$

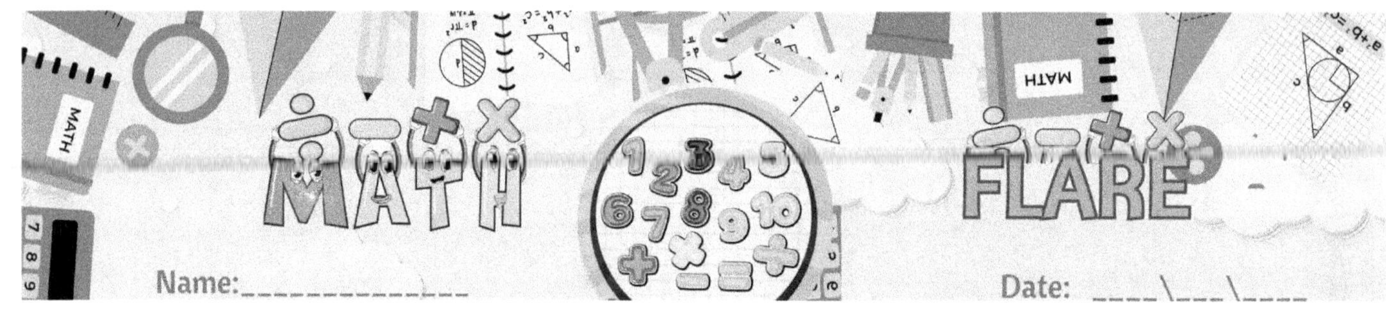

81. $10x + 2 = -18$

86. $5x + -8 = 22$

82. $5x + 0 = -5$

87. $3x + 9 = 30$

83. $-9x + 3 = 93$

88. $-8x + 9 = 89$

84. $-10x + 5 = 105$

89. $-7x + 9 = -12$

85. $-6x + -8 = 46$

90. $-5x + -10 = -25$

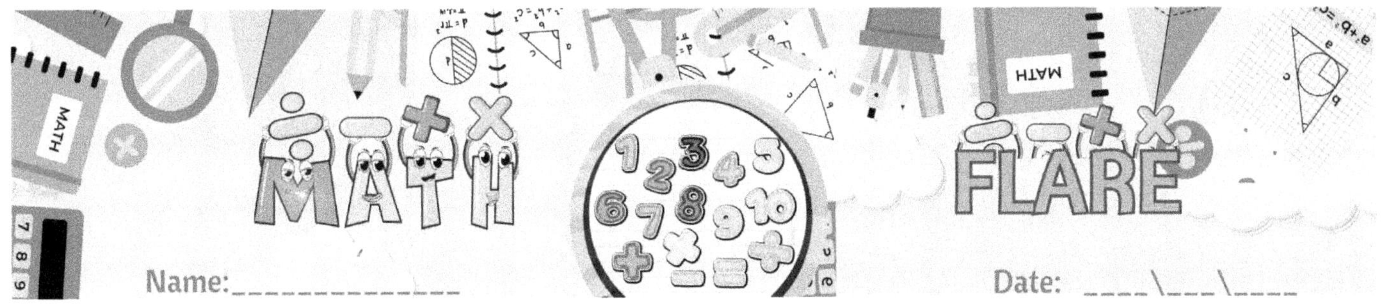

91. $2x + -5 = 11$

96. $9x + -6 = -78$

92. $-4x + 7 = 19$

93. $-4x + -10 = -26$

94. $-5x + -7 = -32$

95. $-9x + -6 = 12$

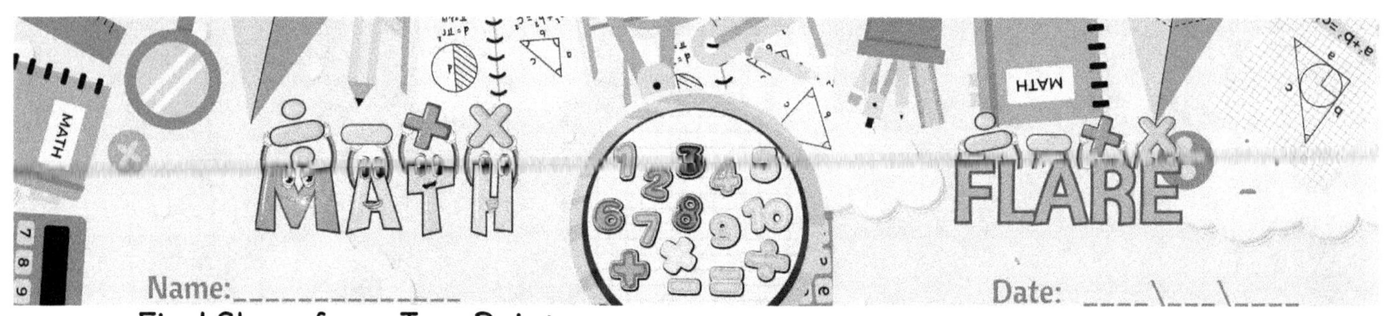

Find Slope from Two Points

1. (1, 2) and (7, 44)

2. (2, 7) and (-2, 7)

3. (-10, -108) and (-4, -48)

4. (9, 1) and (10, 2)

5. (8, -58) and (10, -72)

6. (-8, -66) and (0, 6)

7. (6, -26) and (4, -18)

8. (-7, -12) and (-4, -6)

9. (-6, 51) and (4, -49)

10. (-5, -30) and (-5, -30)

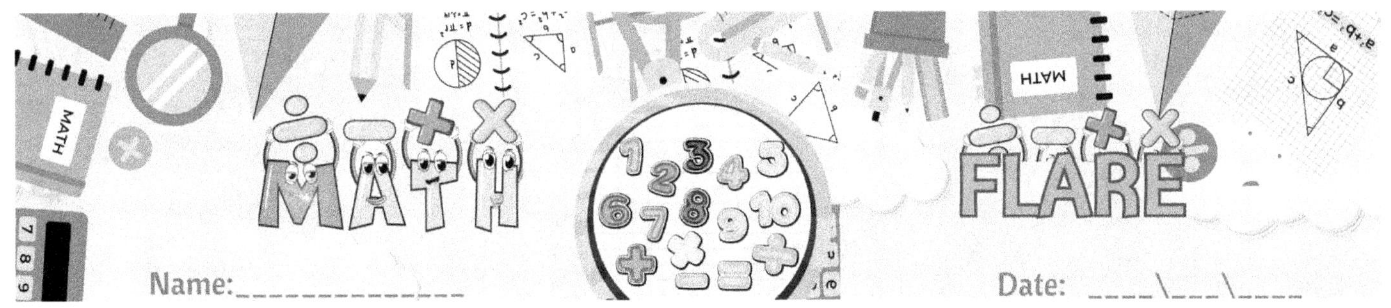

11. (8, 44) and (-8, -36)

12. (-2, -10) and (-8, -10)

13. (7, -28) and (9, -34)

14. (-9, 25) and (6, -20)

15. (3, -39) and (9, -99)

16. (-9, 43) and (-10, 48)

17. (-10, 43) and (-3, 8)

18. (9, 30) and (-10, -27)

19. (-7, 56) and (-1, 14)

20. (-3, 24) and (3, -36)

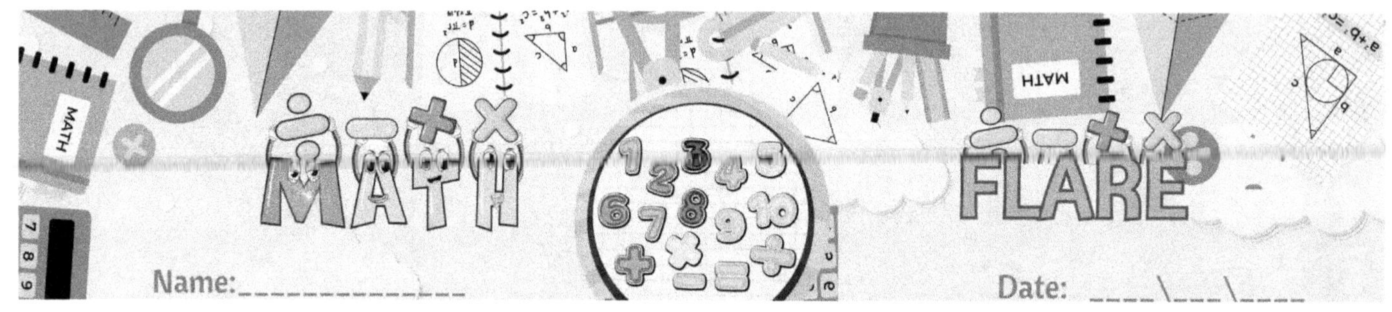

21. (6, -31) and (-4, 29)

22. (0, 2) and (-6, -40)

23. (-8, -7) and (5, 6)

24. (4, 41) and (-2, -19)

25. (-5, -15) and (-4, -12)

26. (-8, -15) and (-10, -19)

27. (2, 28) and (-2, -8)

28. (-4, -26) and (5, 46)

29. (7, 18) and (2, 8)

30. (-8, -79) and (9, 74)

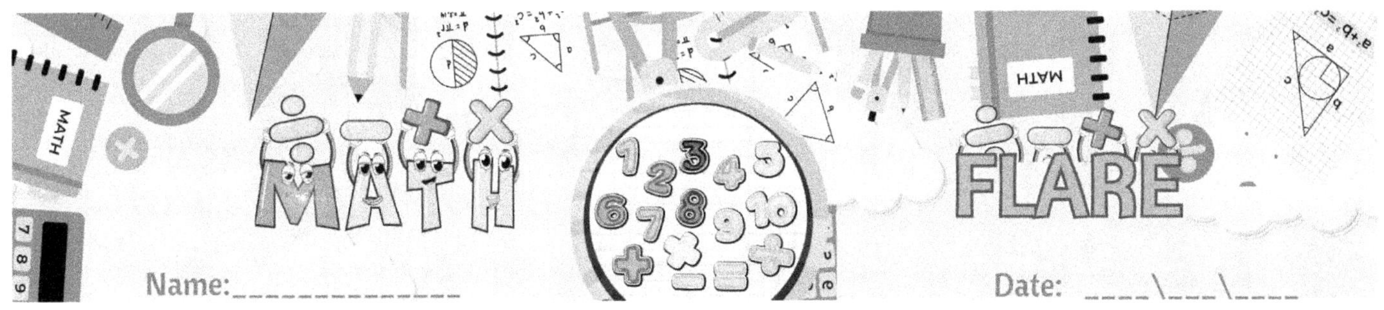

31. (8, -32) and (-1, 4)

32. (8, -64) and (-1, 17)

33. (-7, 53) and (9, -91)

34. (8, 40) and (2, 10)

35. (10, -110) and (5, -60)

36. (5, 17) and (4, 13)

37. (-9, -52) and (-8, -46)

38. (-7, 51) and (-9, 63)

39. (0, 1) and (-6, 31)

40. (-10, 78) and (10, -62)

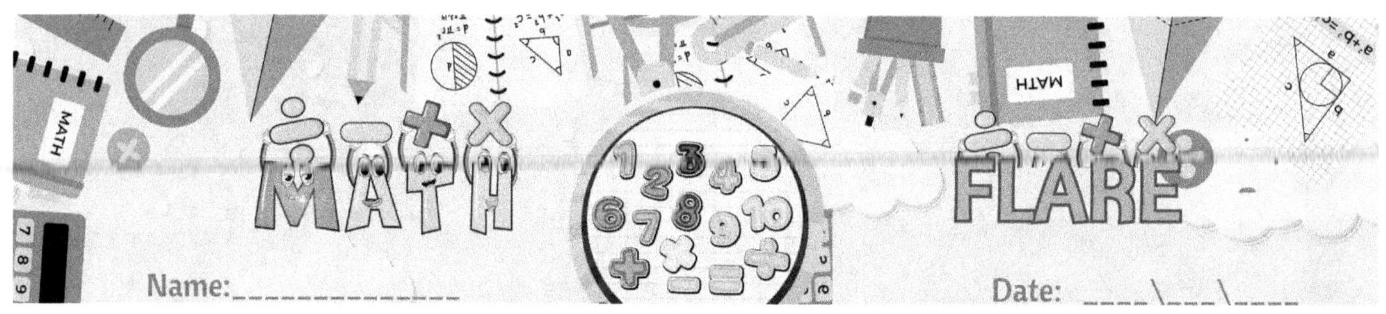

41. (1, -4) and (3, 4)

46. (10, -106) and (4, -46)

42. (-3, -14) and (-9, -44)

47. (-1, -11) and (9, -1)

43. (-1, 13) and (5, -17)

48. (2, -12) and (6, -24)

44. (5, 46) and (6, 55)

49. (-2, -1) and (-8, 11)

45. (8, 37) and (-9, -31)

50. (-4, 17) and (-7, 29)

Name:_______________   Date: _______________

Plotting Lines

1.

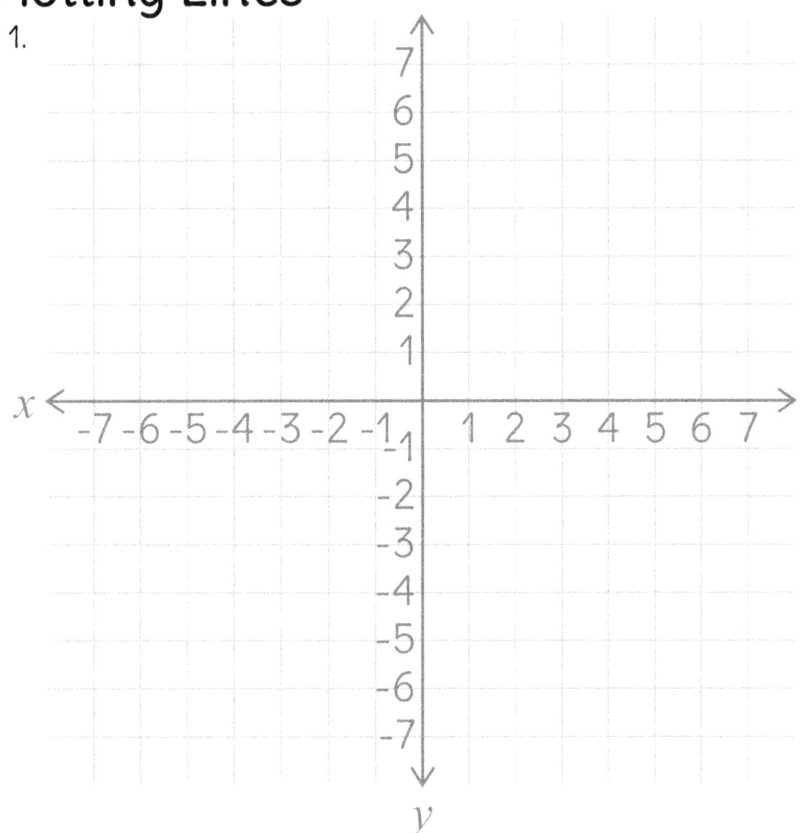

A = (1, -1)   B = (-7, 7)

C = (7, -7)   D = (6, -6)

E = (-5, 5)   F = (-2, 2)

2.

A = (5, -1)   B = (2, -1)

C = (-7, -1)   D = (0, -1)

E = (-2, -1)   F = (-4, -1)

Name:_________________   Date: ______________

3.

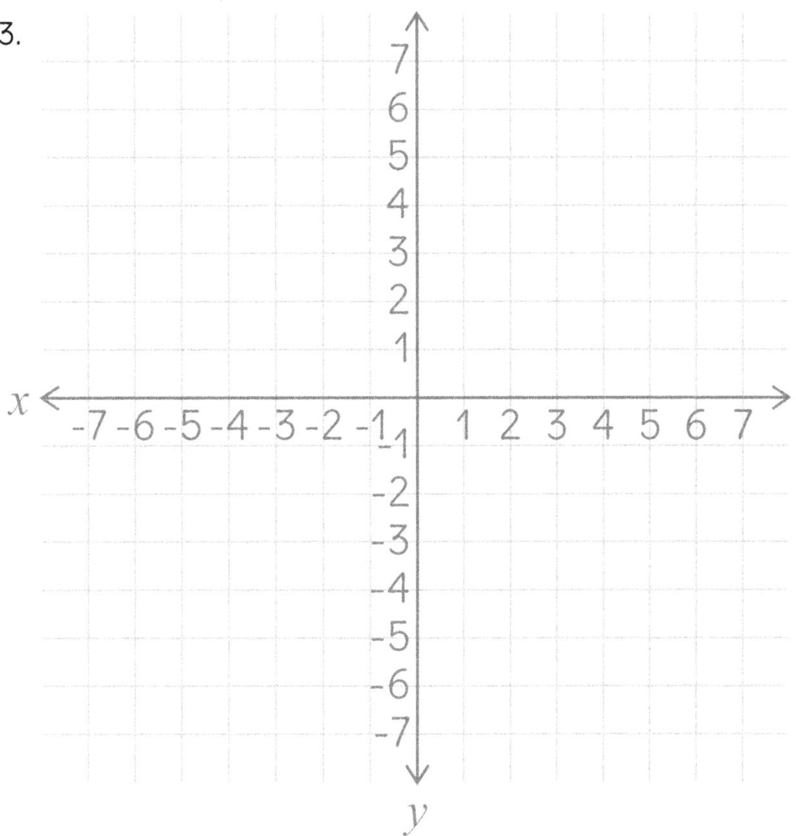

A = (-2, -5)   B = (-3, -5)

C = (4, -5)   D = (2, -5)

E = (-6, -5)   F = (-1, -5)

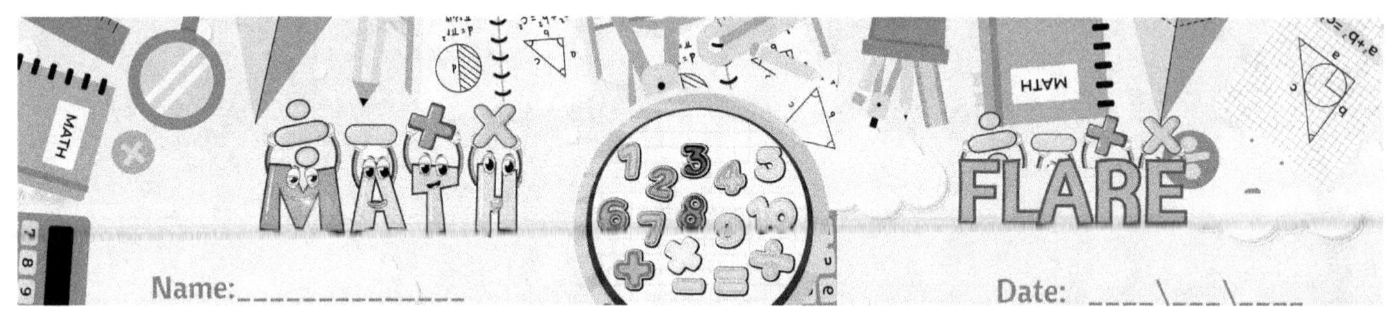

4.

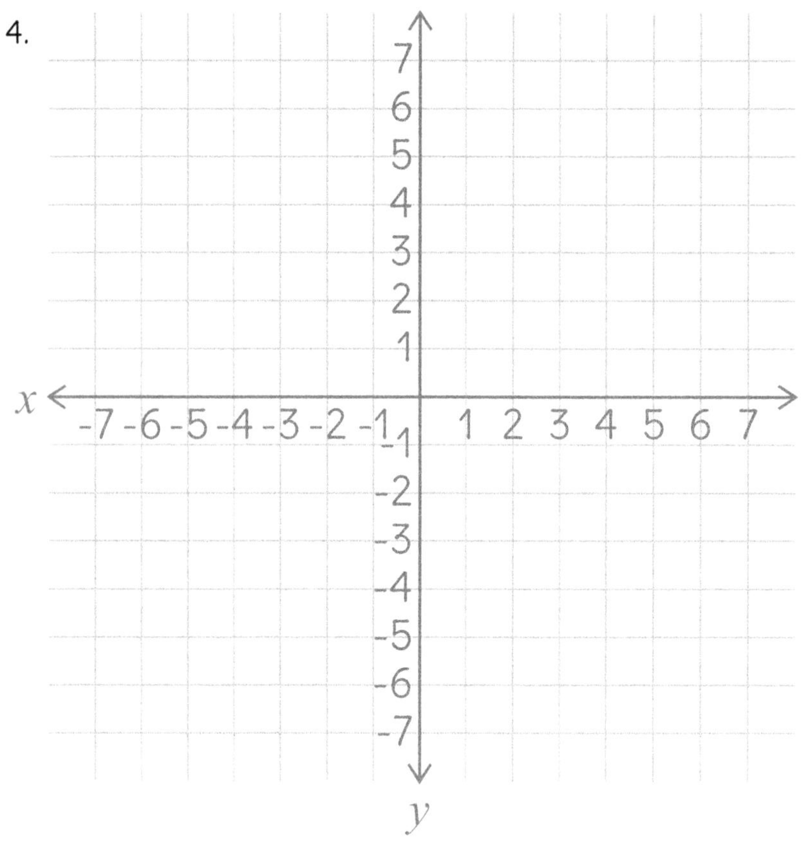

A = (-7, -3)   B = (1, 5)

C = (-6, -2)   D = (-1, 3)

E = (-5, -1)   F = (0, 4)

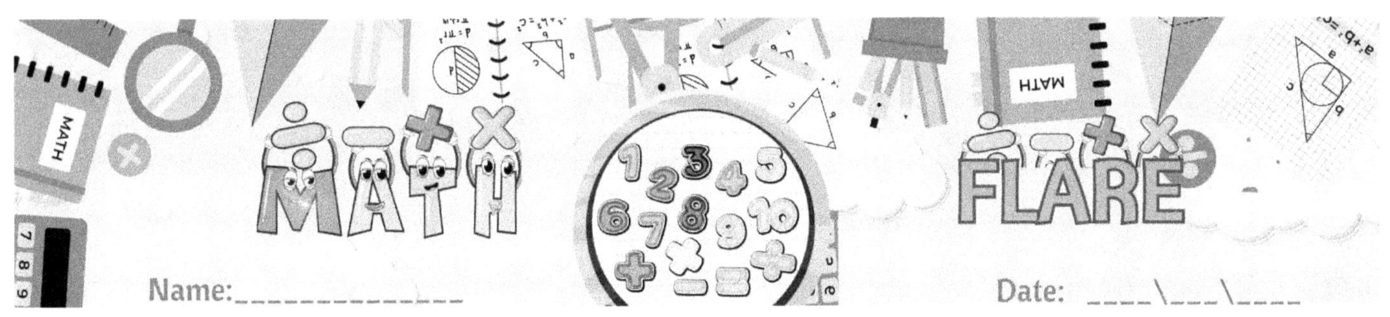

5.

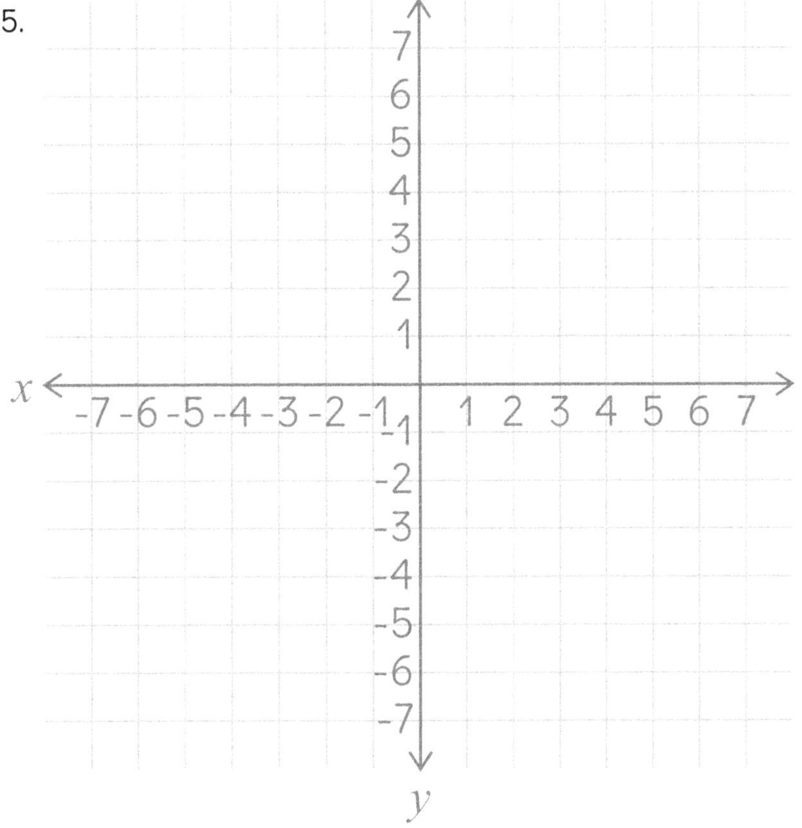

A = (6, -2)   B = (-3, 7)

C = (7, -3)   D = (-1, 5)

E = (5, -1)   F = (3, 1)

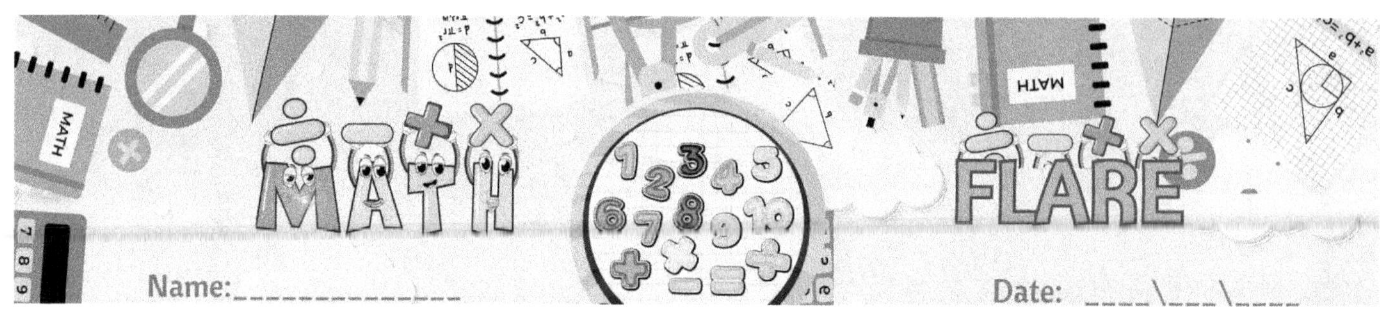

6.

A = (3, -7)   B = (-6, -7)

C = (-4, -7)   D = (7, -7)

E = (6, -7)   F = (5, -7)

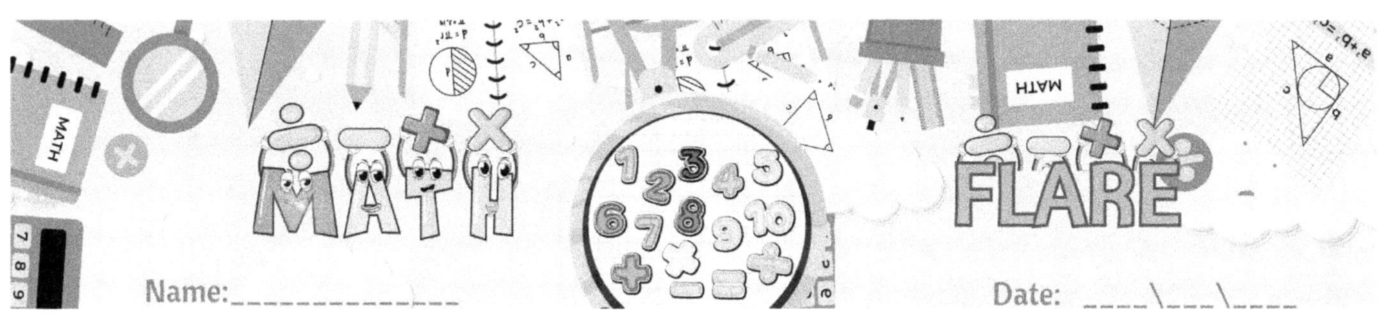

7.

$$A = (-4, -2) \qquad B = (-1, 1)$$

$$C = (3, 5) \qquad D = (-5, -3)$$

$$E = (2, 4) \qquad F = (-2, 0)$$

8.

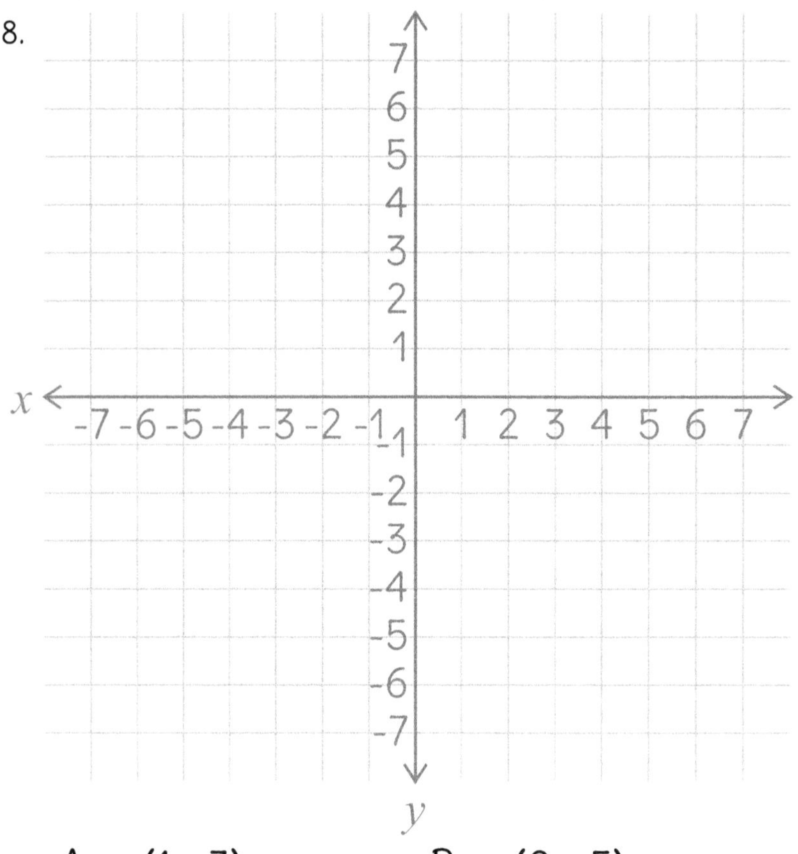

A = (1, -3)   B = (0, -5)

C = (2, -1)   D = (-1, -7)

E = (4, 3)   F = (5, 5)

9.

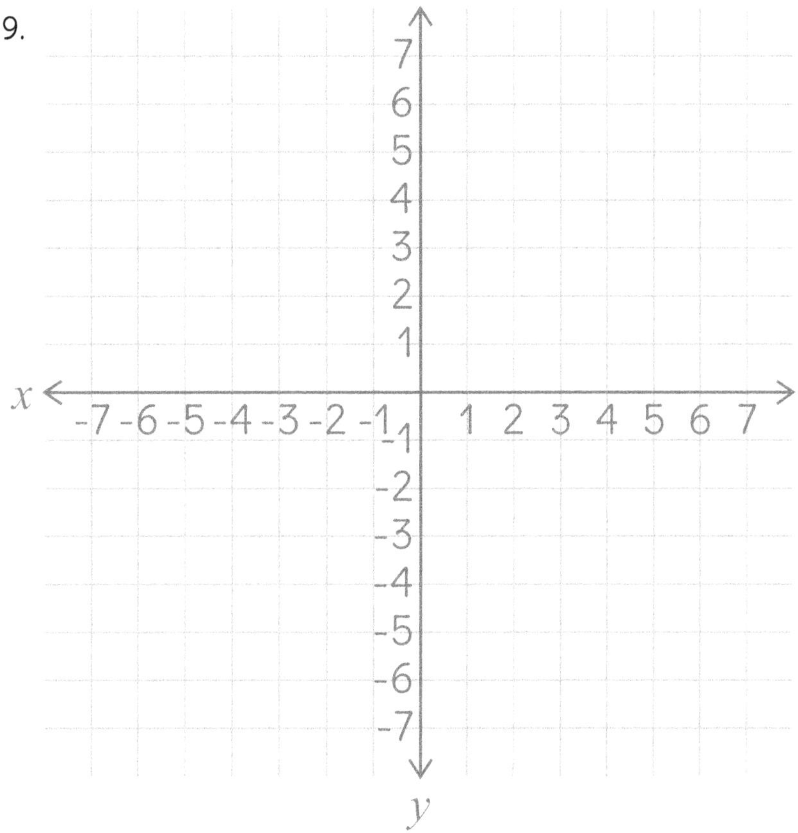

A = (-3, 6)   B = (1, -2)

C = (2, -4)   D = (3, -6)

E = (-1, 2)   F = (0, 0)

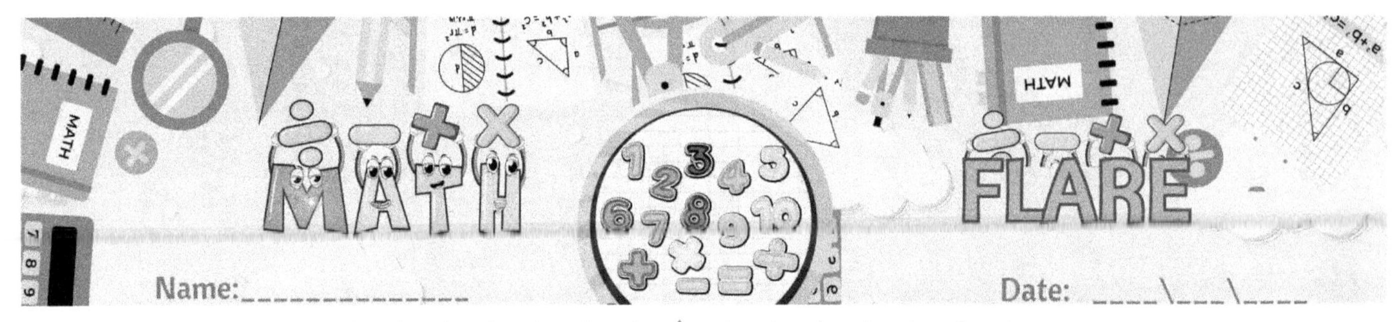

10.

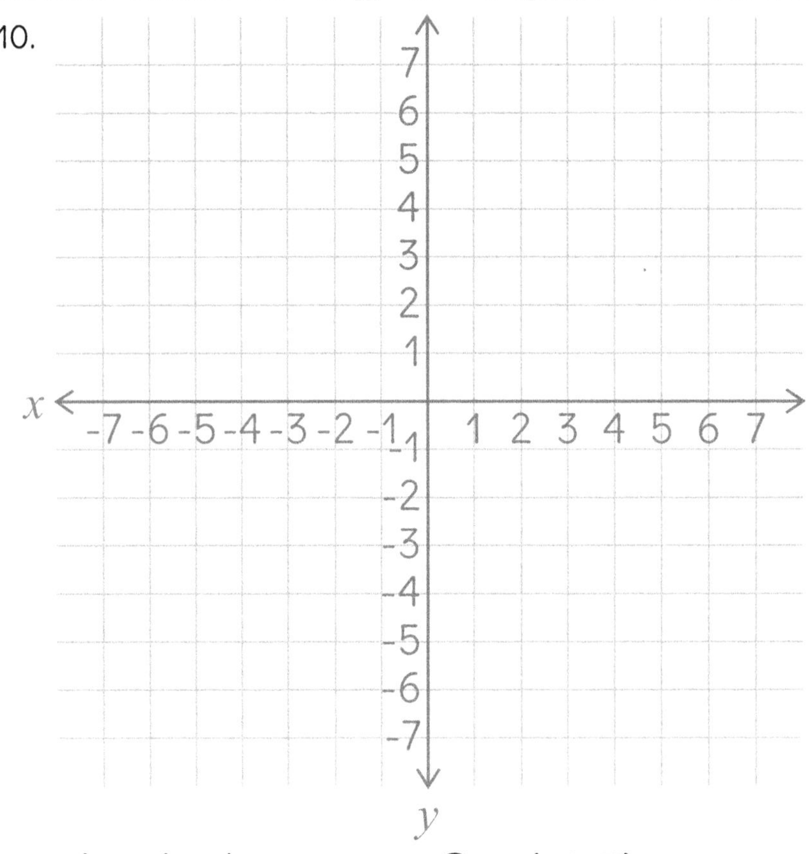

A = (1, 3)   B = (-4, 3)

C = (-3, 3)   D = (7, 3)

E = (-1, 3)   F = (6, 3)

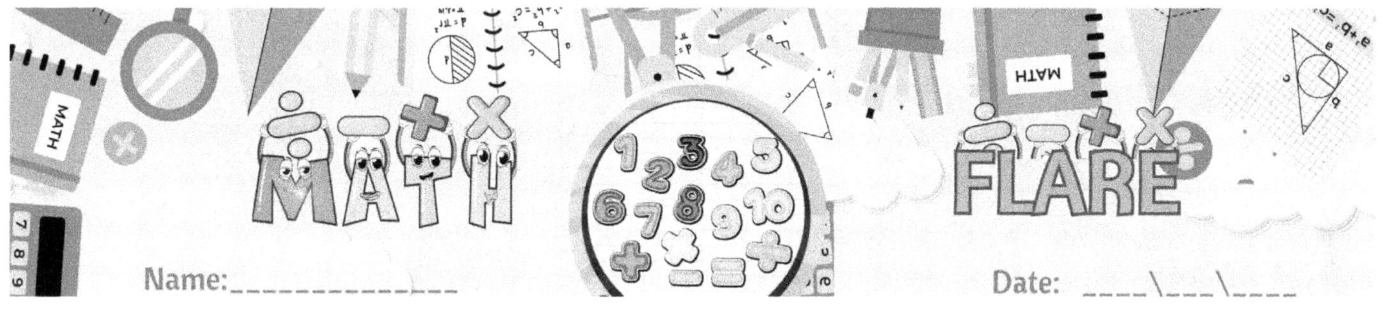

Graphing Linear Equations

1. 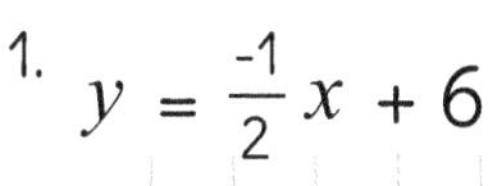
$$y = \frac{-1}{2}x + 6$$

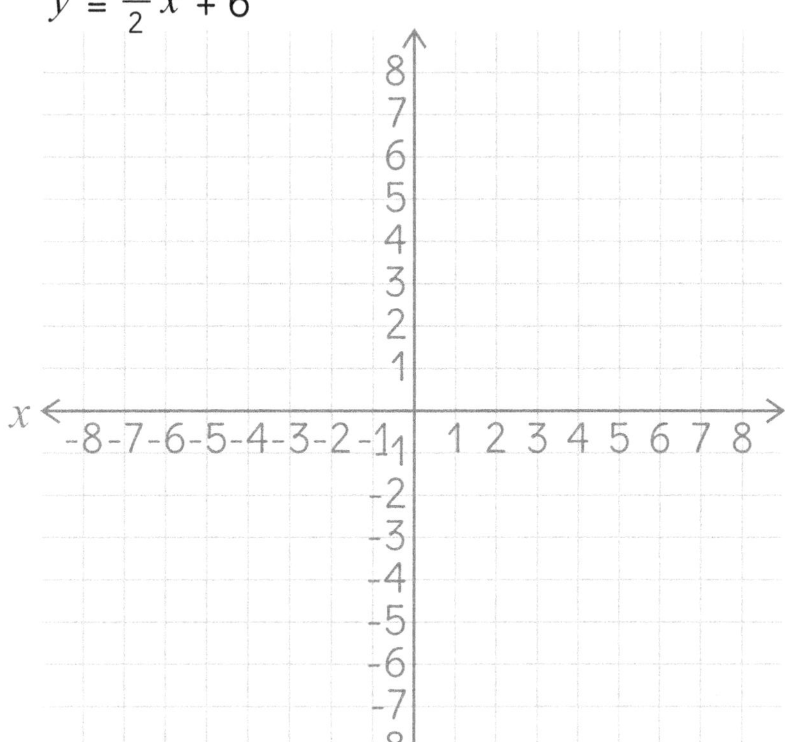

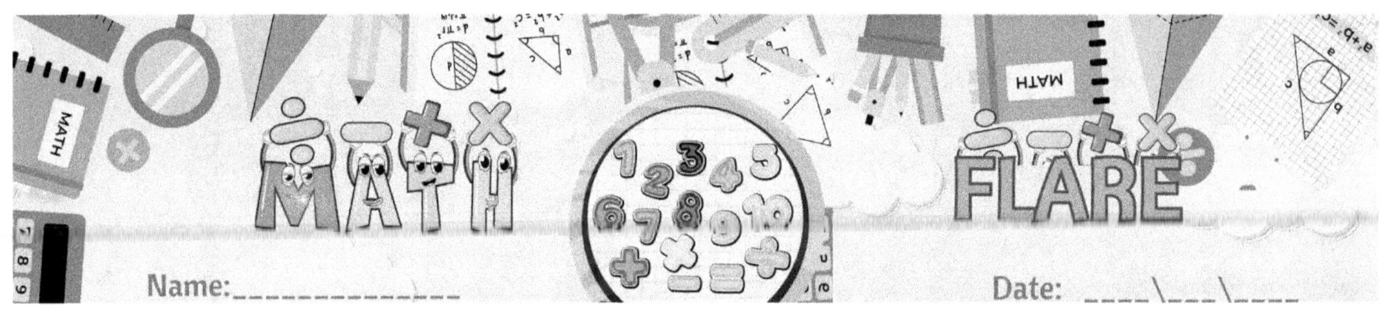

2. $y = \dfrac{3}{4} x$

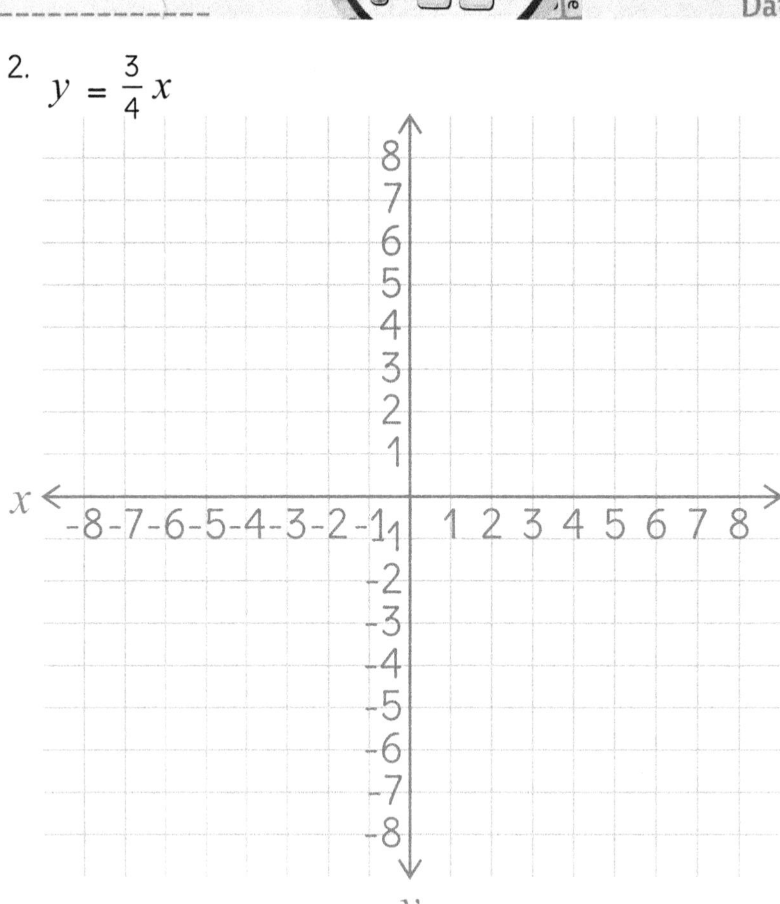

MATH
FLARE
MATH
MATH
Name:________________
Date: _______________

3. $x = 6$

x
y
-8 -7 -6 -5 -4 -3 -2 -1
1 2 3 4 5 6 7 8
8 7 6 5 4 3 2 1
-2 -3 -4 -5 -6 -7 -8

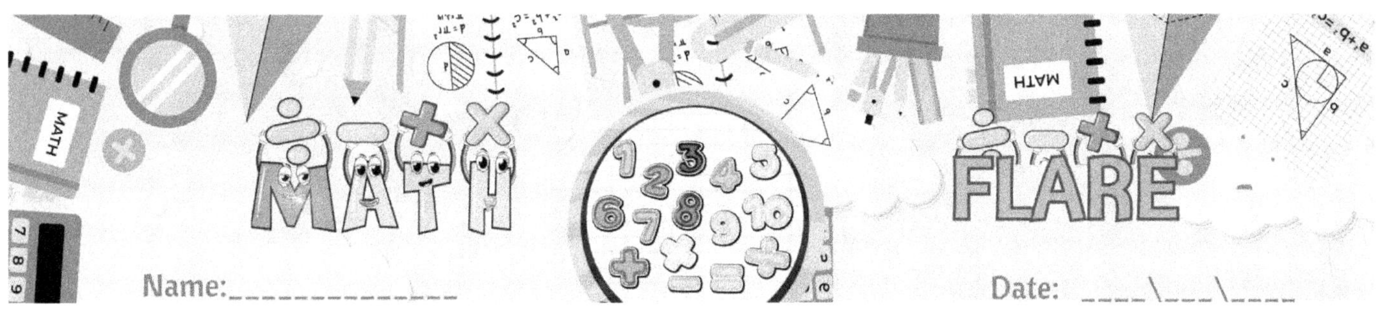

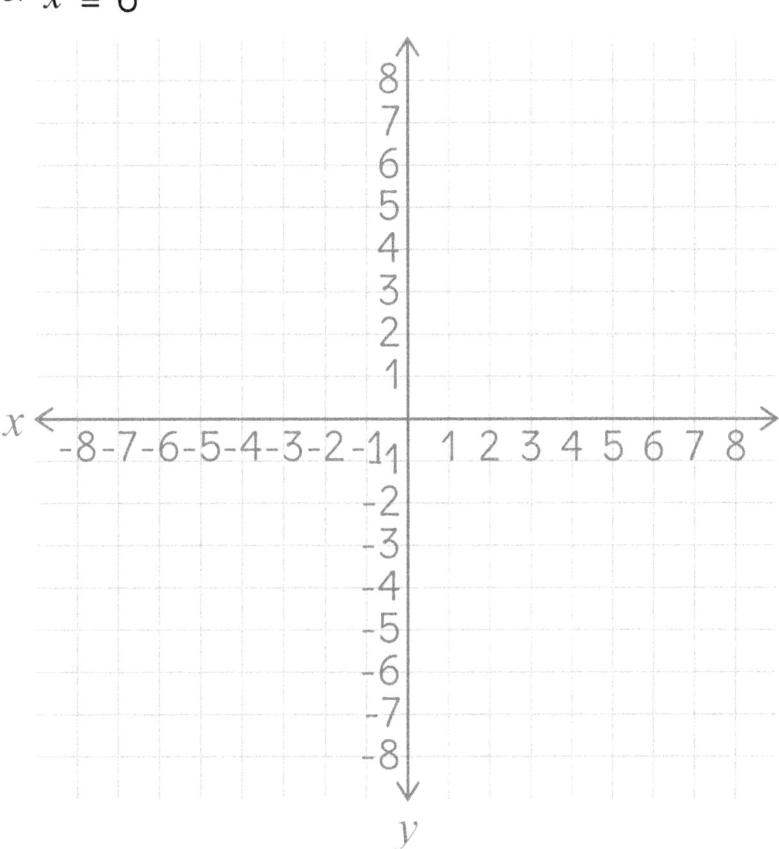

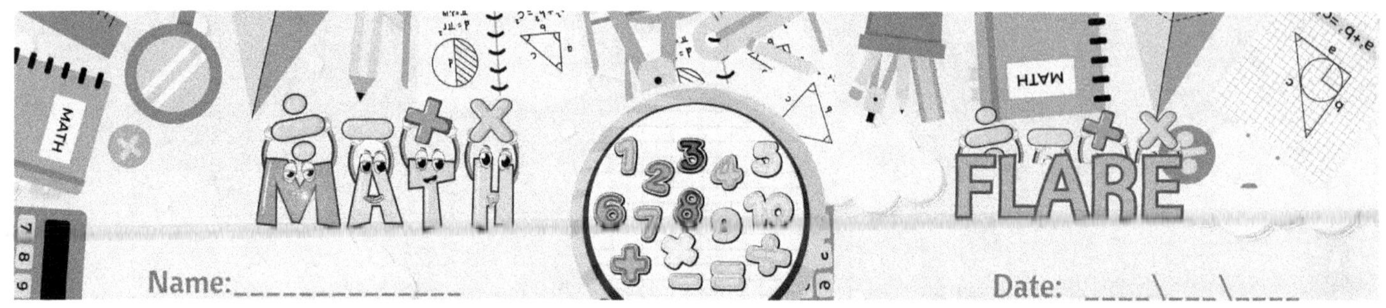

4. $y = \dfrac{-11}{4}x + 3$

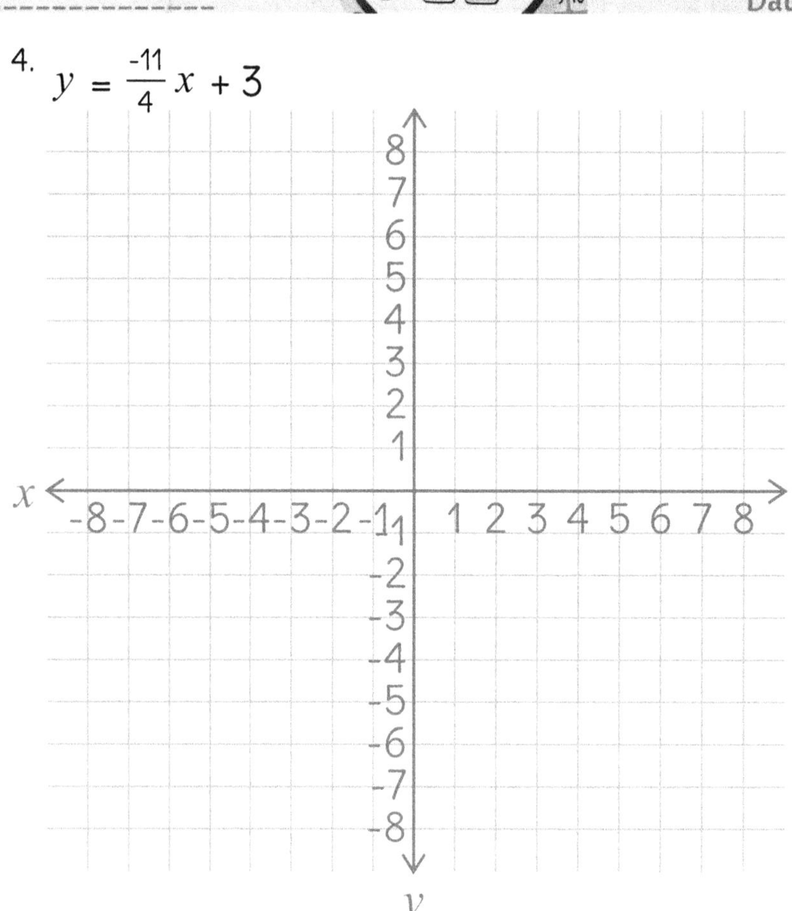

Name:_________________   Date: _______________

5. $y = x - 5$

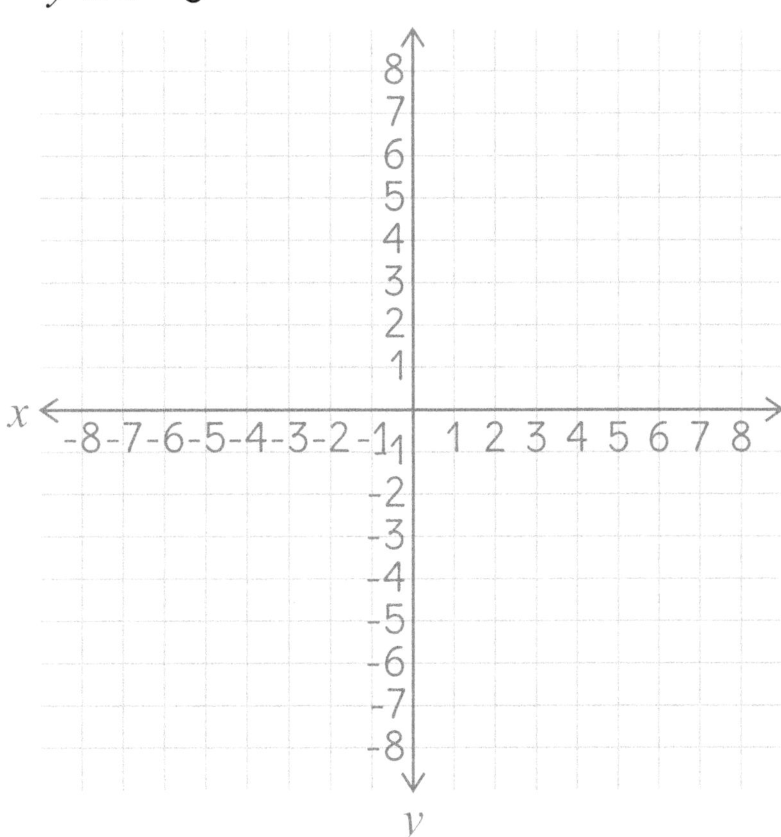

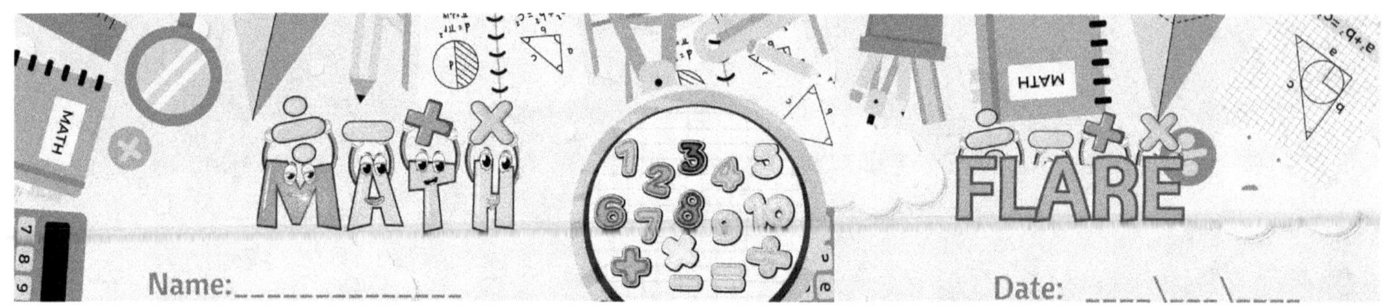

6.

$$y = -2x + 5$$

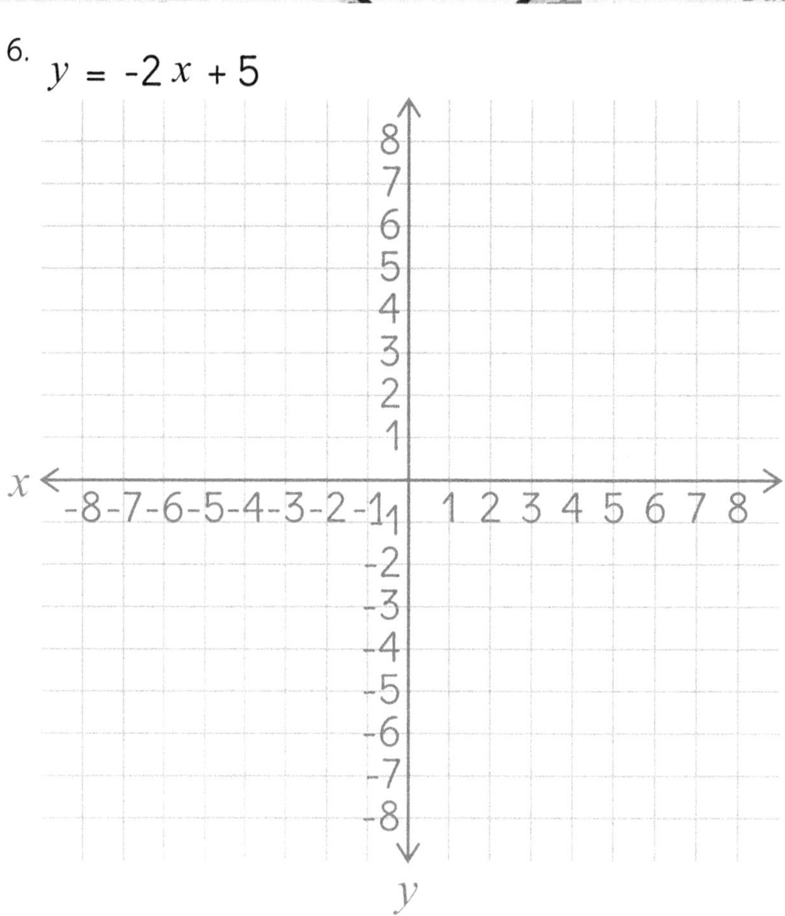

7. $y = \dfrac{-11}{4}x - 4$

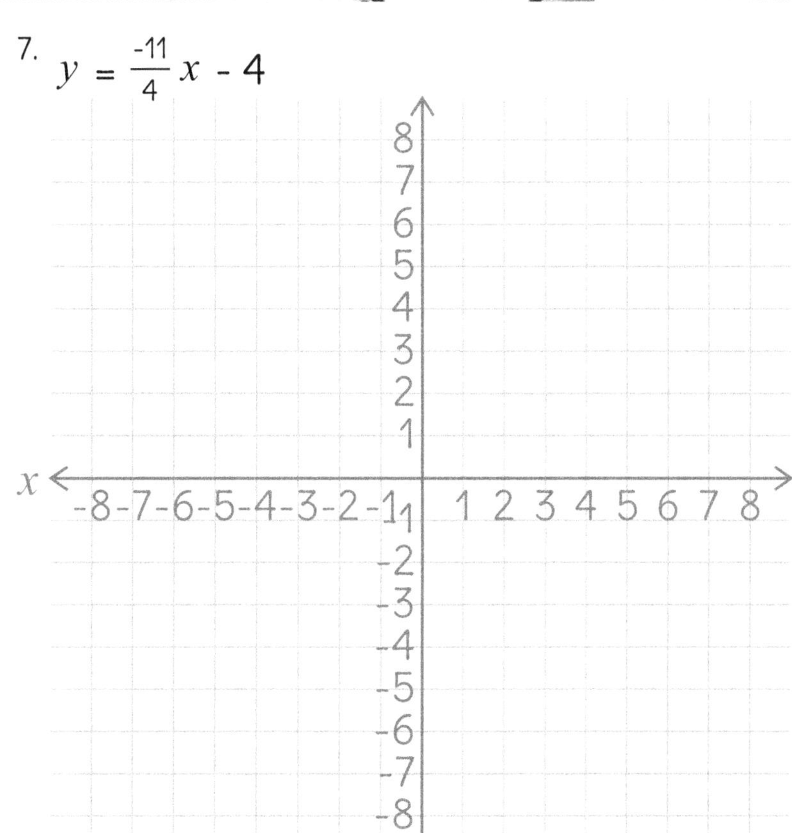

MATH FLARE
Name:________________
Date: ____________

8.
$$y = -2x + 2$$

x
-8-7-6-5-4-3-2-1 1 2 3 4 5 6 7 8
8 7 6 5 4 3 2 1 -2 -3 -4 -5 -6 -7 -8
y

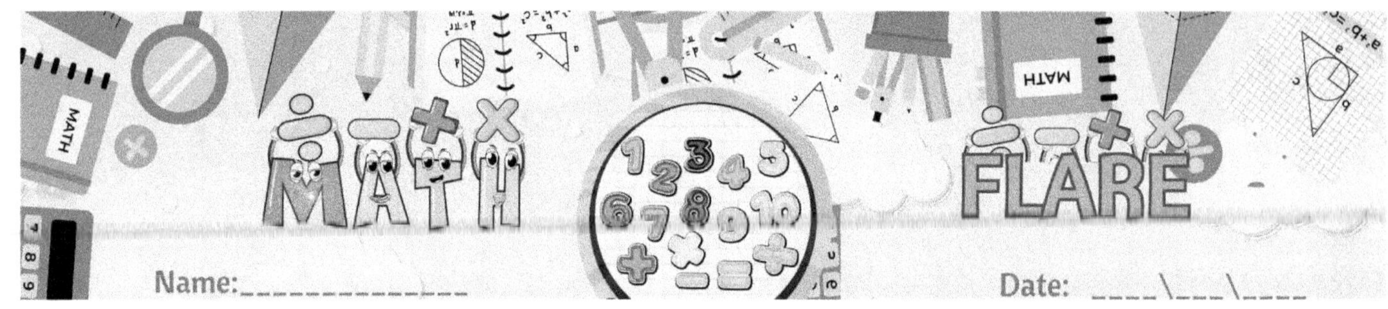

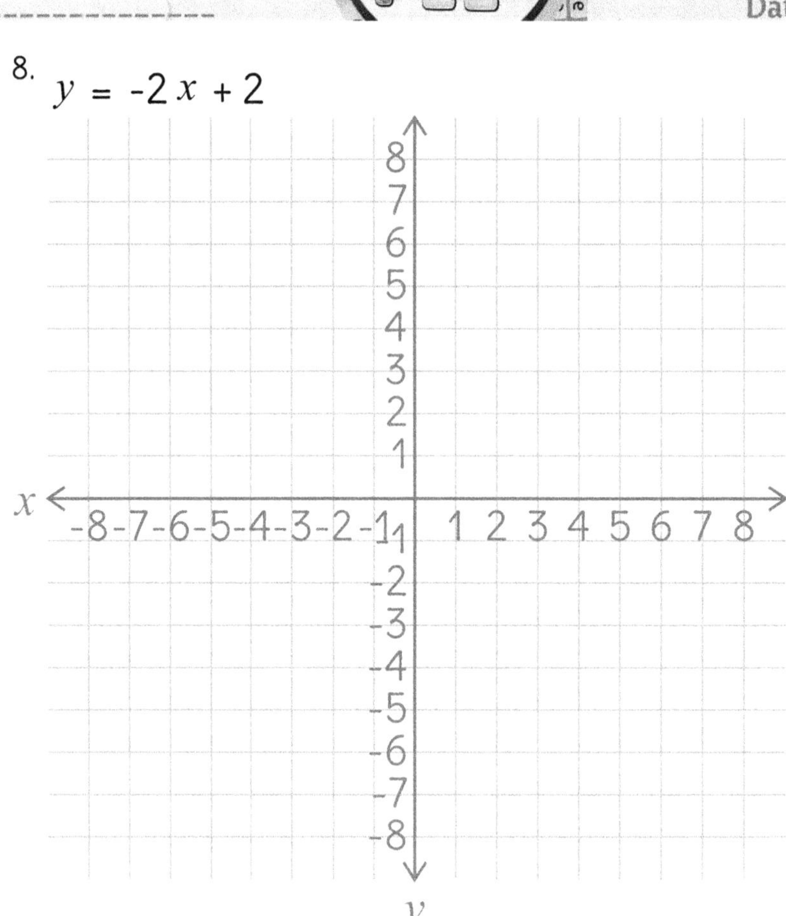

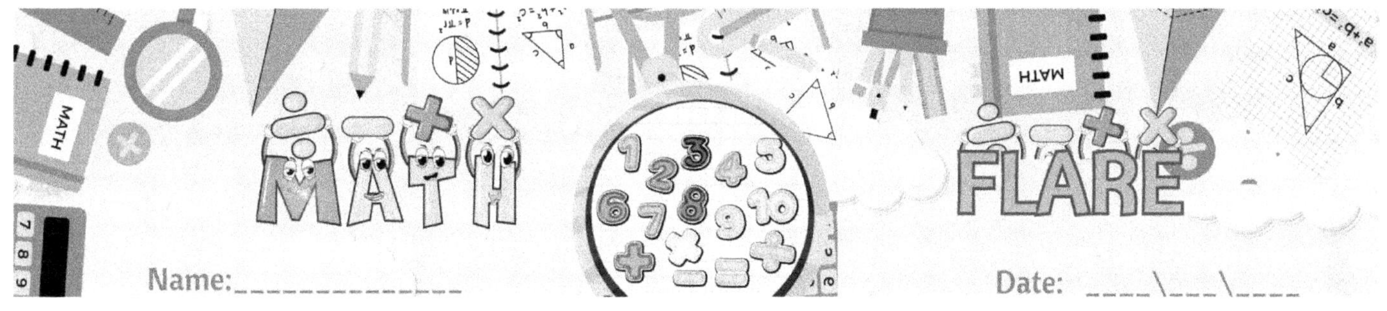

Name:_______________   Date: _______________

9.
$$y = \frac{1}{2}x - 8$$

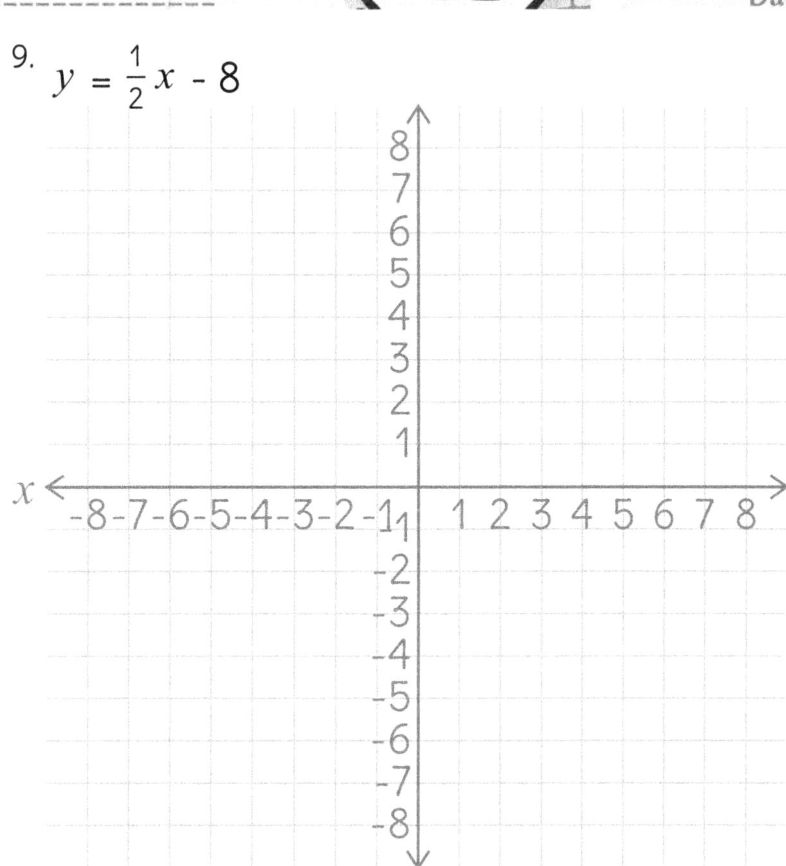

10.
$$y = 2x + 7$$

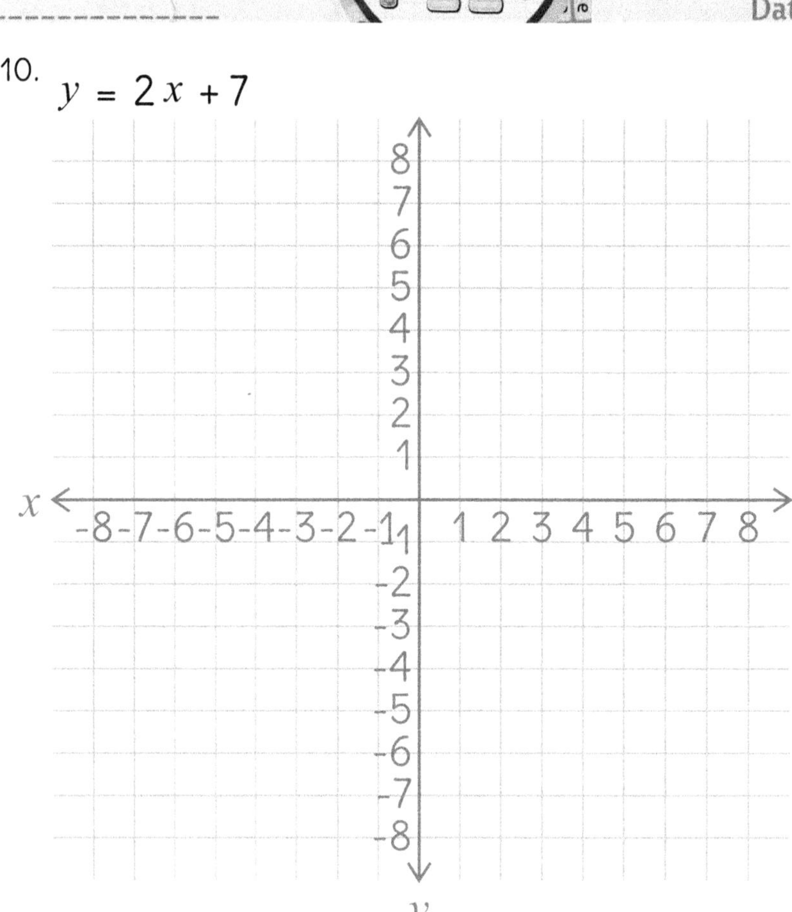

11.
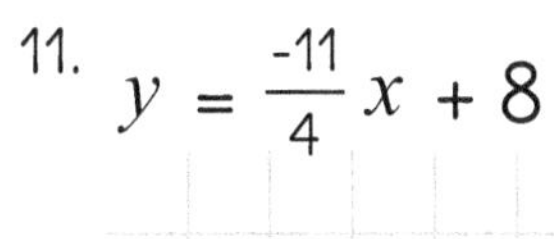

$$y = \frac{-11}{4}x + 8$$

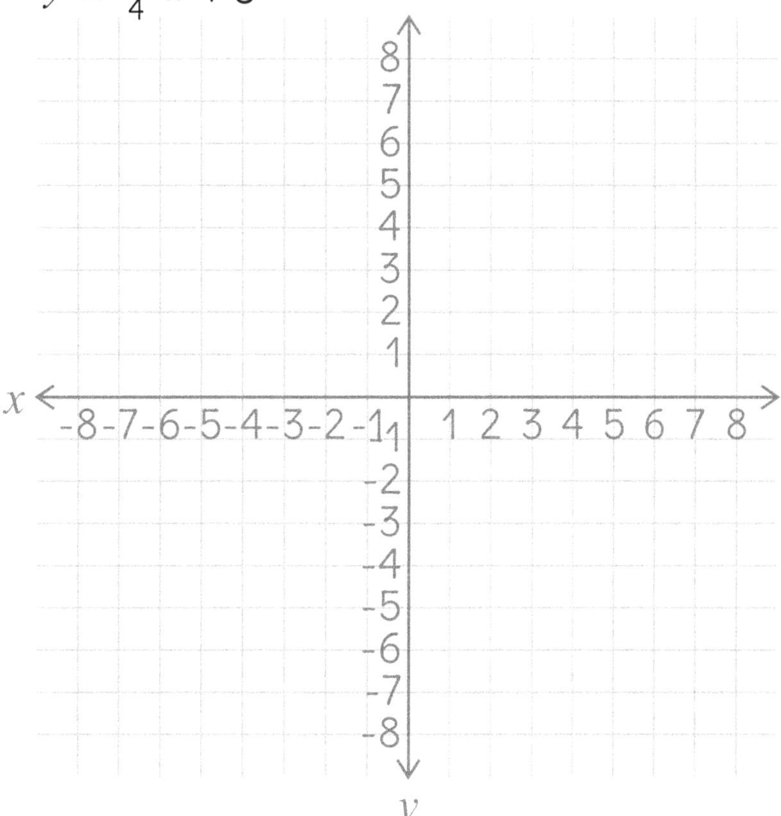

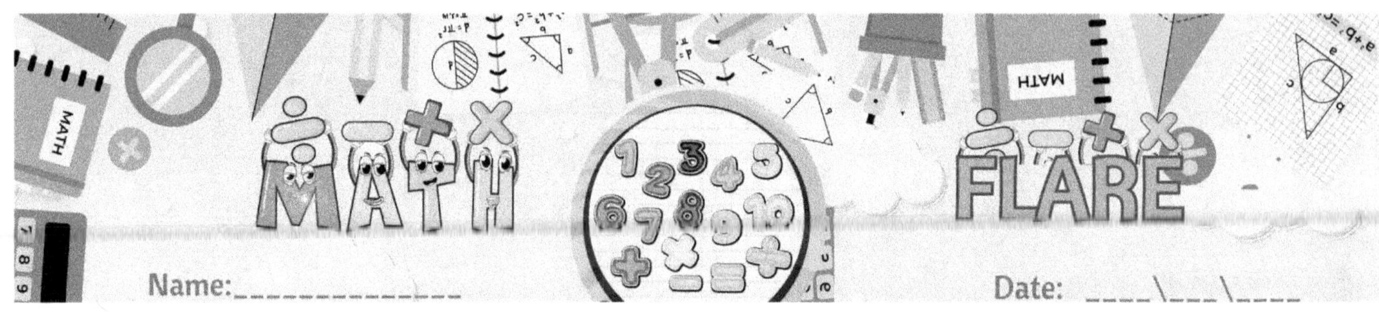

12. $y = \dfrac{-9}{4}x + 7$

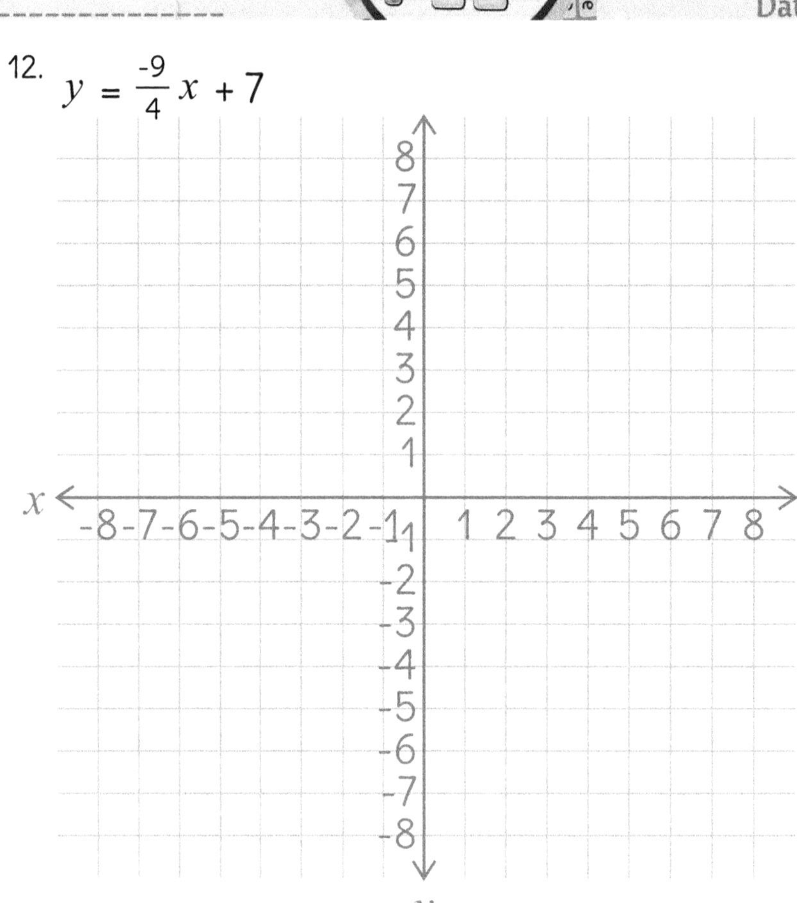

Name:_______________   Date: _____________

13. 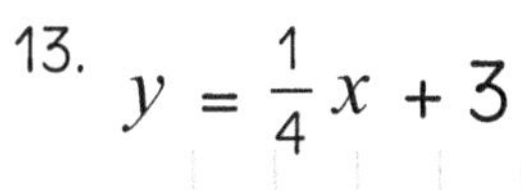

$$y = \frac{1}{4}x + 3$$

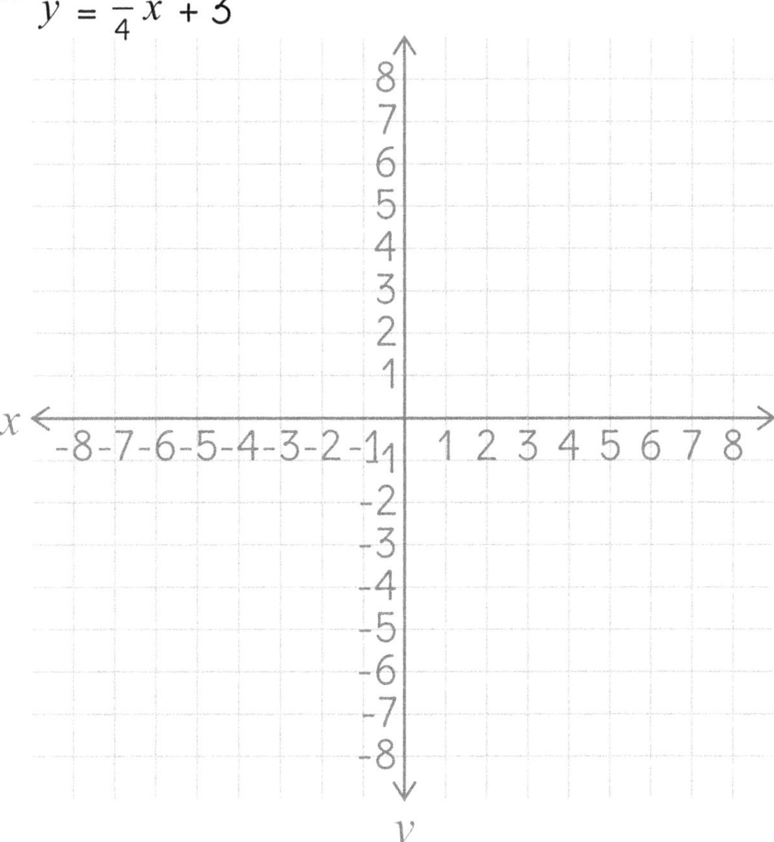

Name:_______________ Date: ____________

14. $y = \dfrac{-1}{2} x + 7$

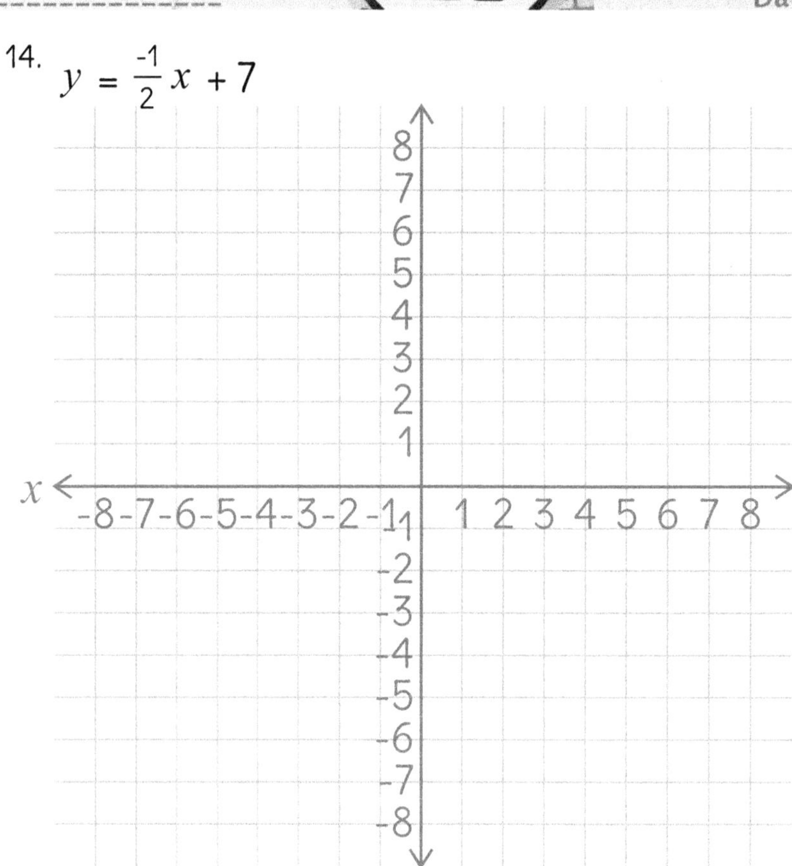

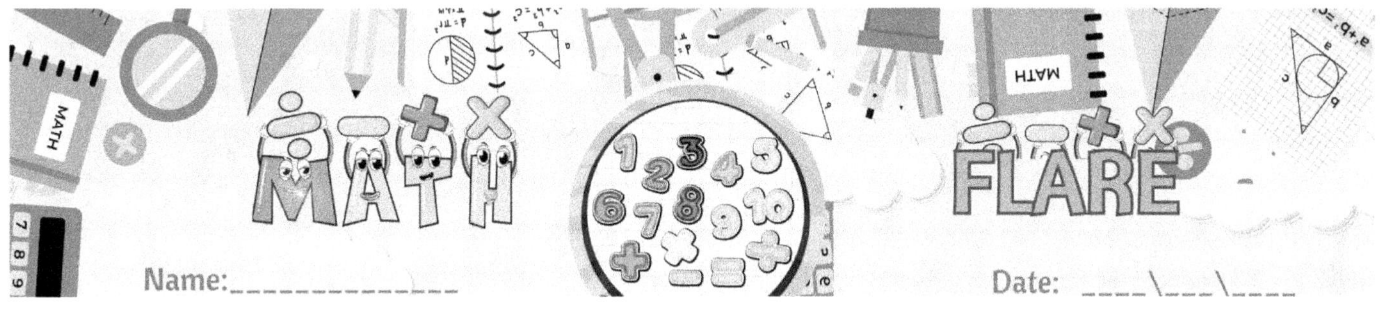

15. $y = \dfrac{7}{4}x + 8$

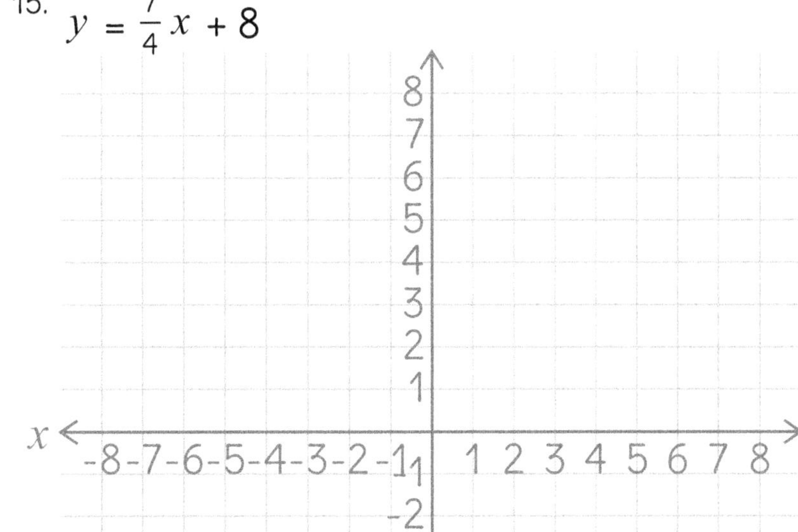

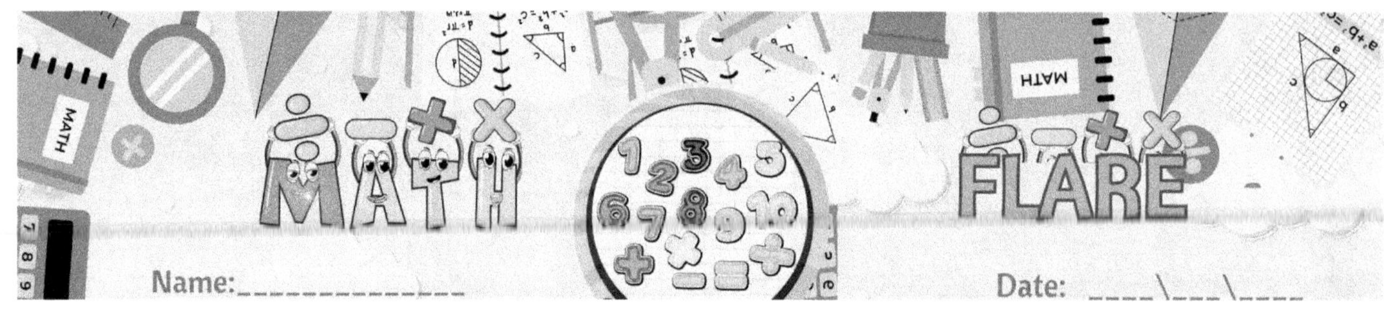

16.

$$y = \frac{3}{4}x - 1$$

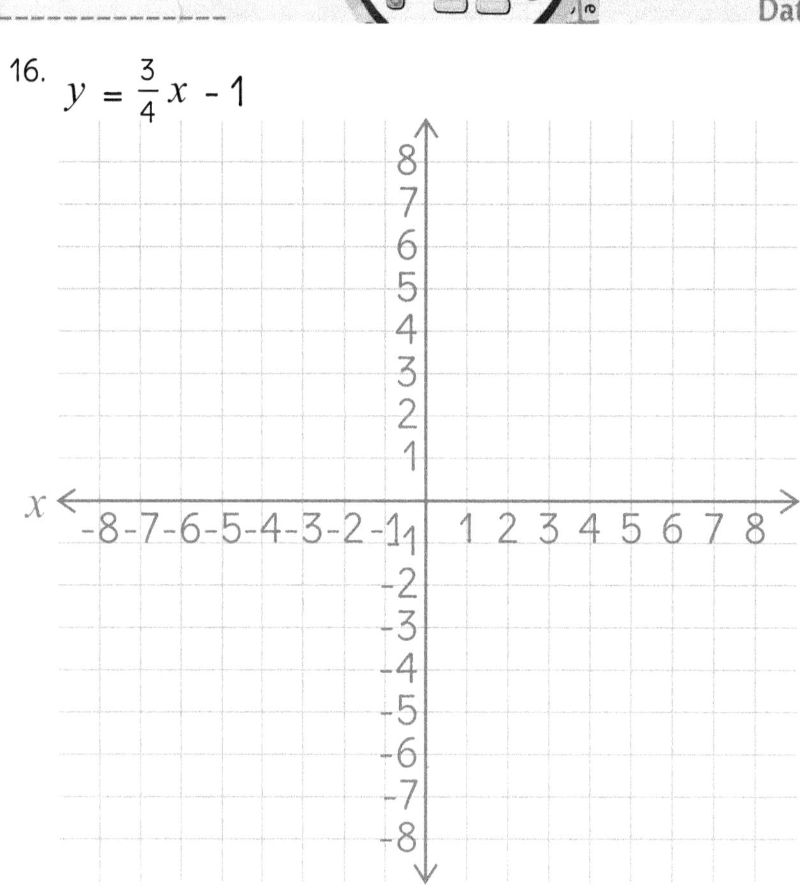

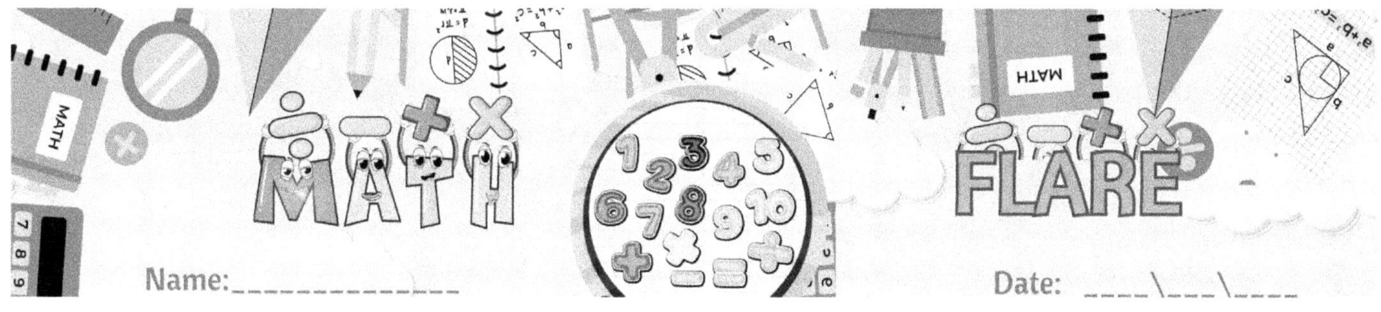

17.
$$y = \frac{3}{2}x + 3$$

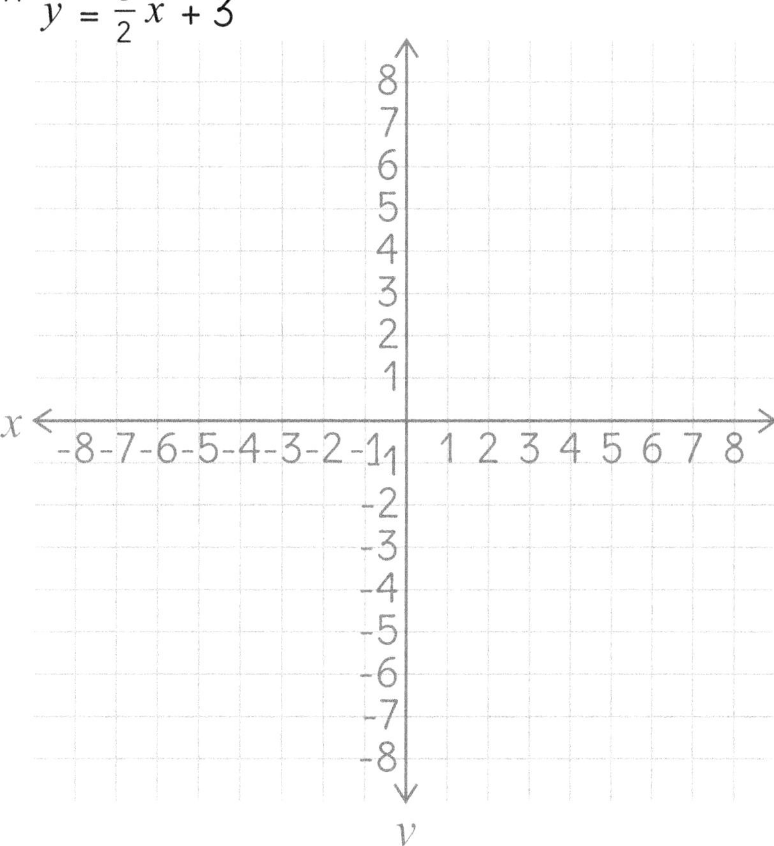

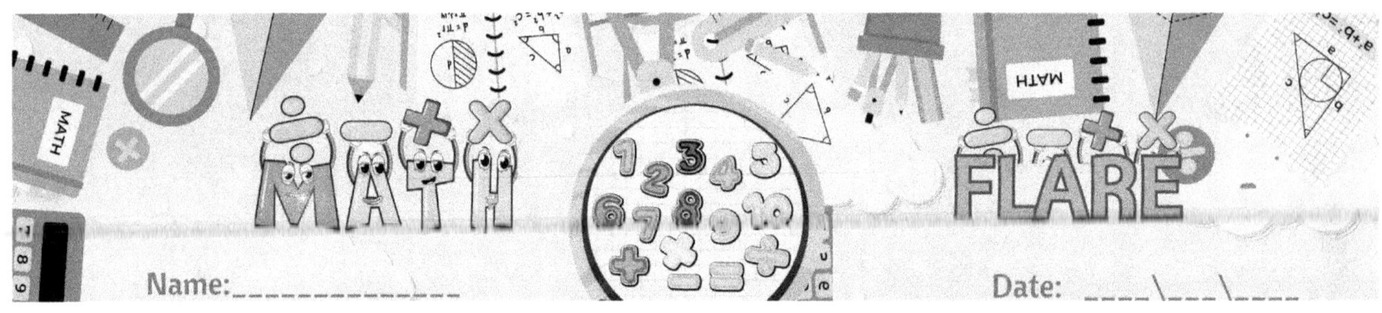

18.
$$y = \frac{11}{4}x - 1$$

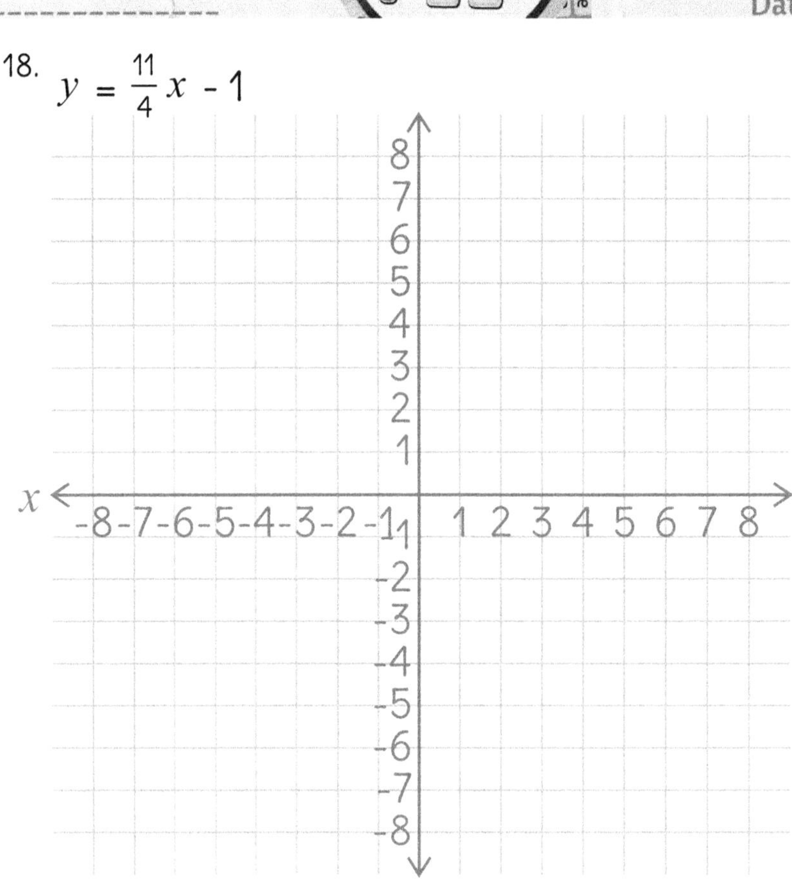

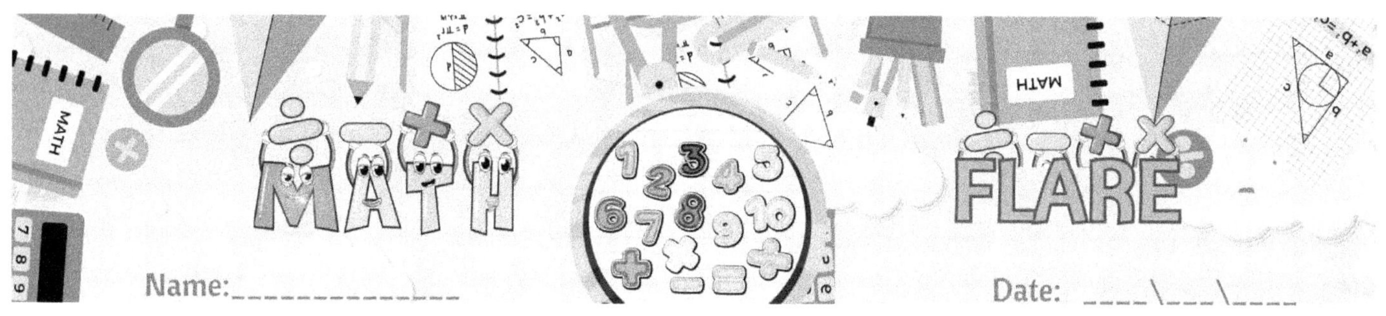

19.
$$y = -2x + 1$$

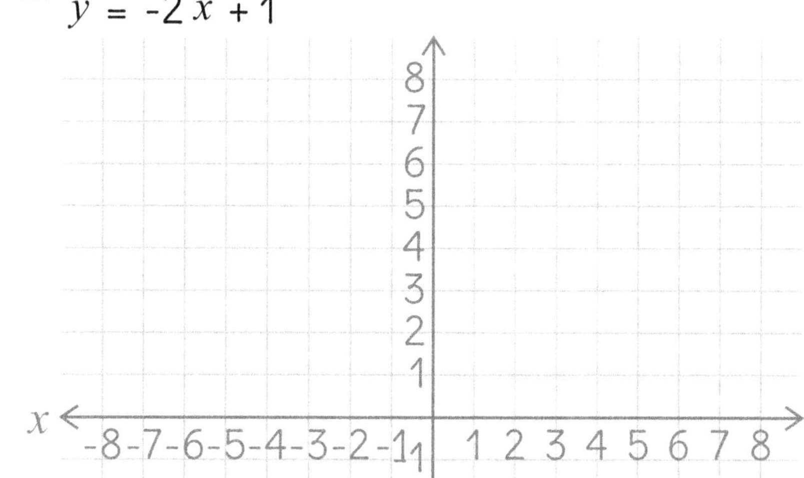

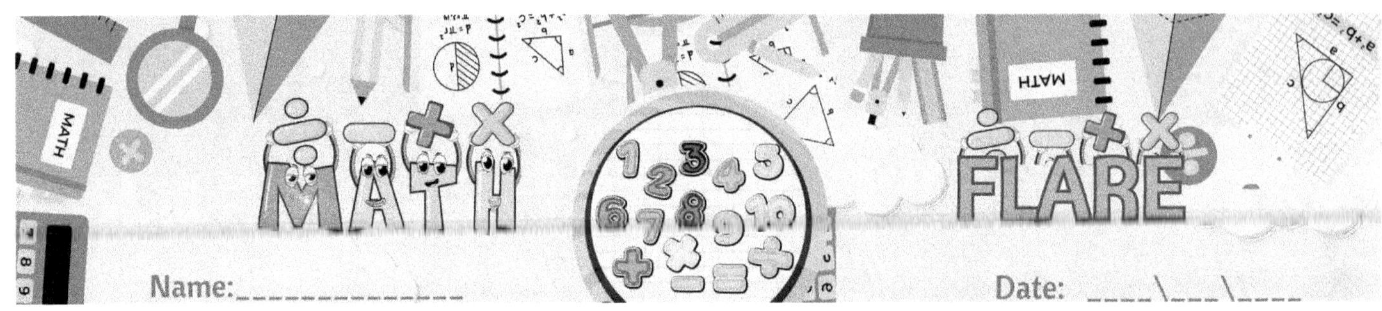

20.
$$y = -3x - 3$$

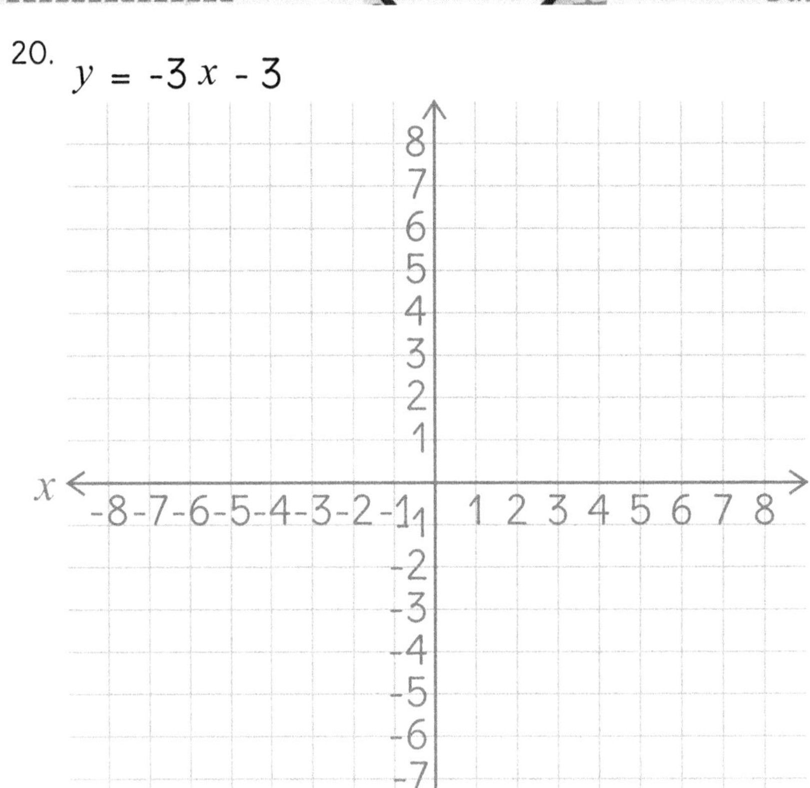

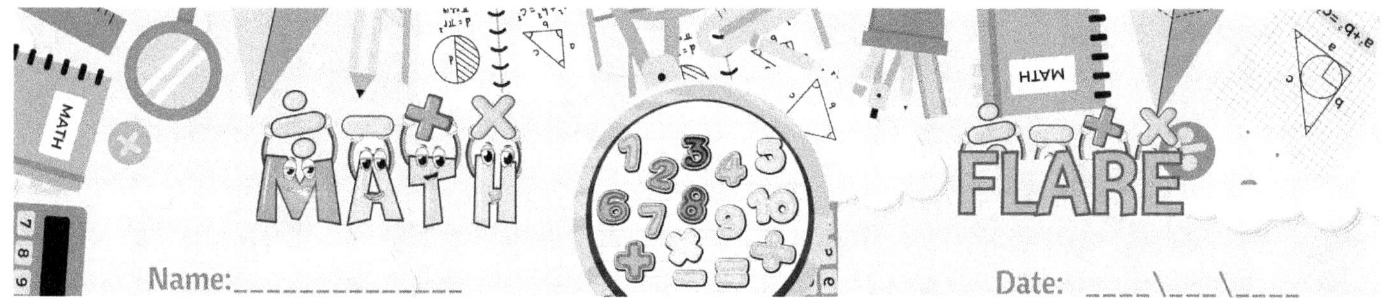

Name:______________ Date: _______________

System of Equations

1. $3x + 9y = 3$

   $5x + 4y = 6$

2. $9x + 3y = 2$

   $2x + 7y = 1$

3. $7x + 2y = 8$

   $8x + 4y = 1$

4. $2x + 8y = 10$

   $7x + 9y = 4$

5. $10x + 5y = 9$

   $9x + 4y = 6$

6. $6x + 5y = 2$

   $7x + 5y = 3$

7. 9x + 4y = 6

   2x + 1y = 4

8. 1x + 6y = 2

   5x + 3y = 4

9. 4x + 7y = 6

   6x + 10y = 9

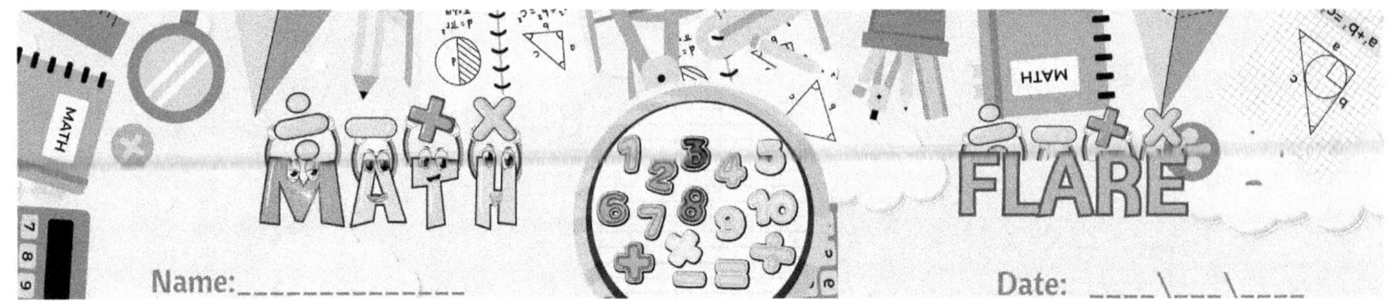

10. $3x + 8y = 1$

   $3x + 10y = 2$

11. $4x + 10y = 9$

   $3x + 8y = 10$

12. $2x + 3y = 3$

   $7x + 8y = 3$

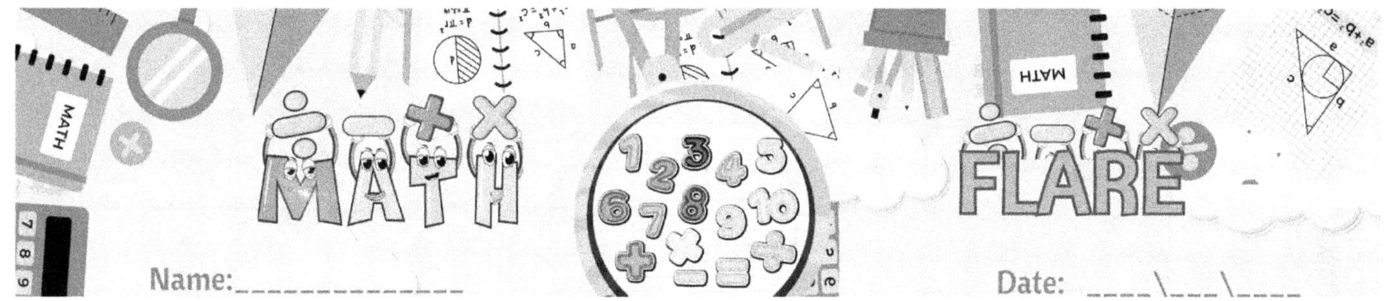

13. $2x + 2y = 10$

$7x + 1y = 9$

14. $4x + 3y = 3$

$9x + 4y = 2$

15. $2x + 5y = 3$

$2x + 8y = 3$

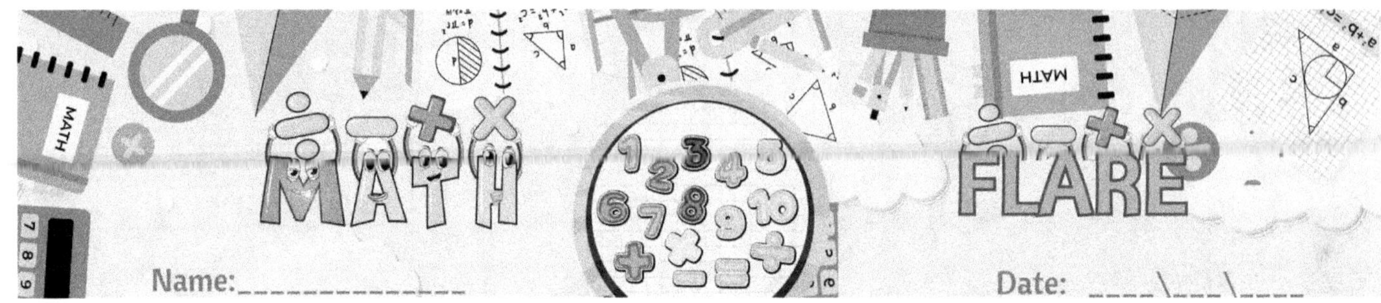

16. $6x + 5y = 7$

$7x + 9y = 8$

17. $1x + 4y = 1$

$5x + 1y = 5$

18. $7x + 10y = 1$

$9x + 1y = 5$

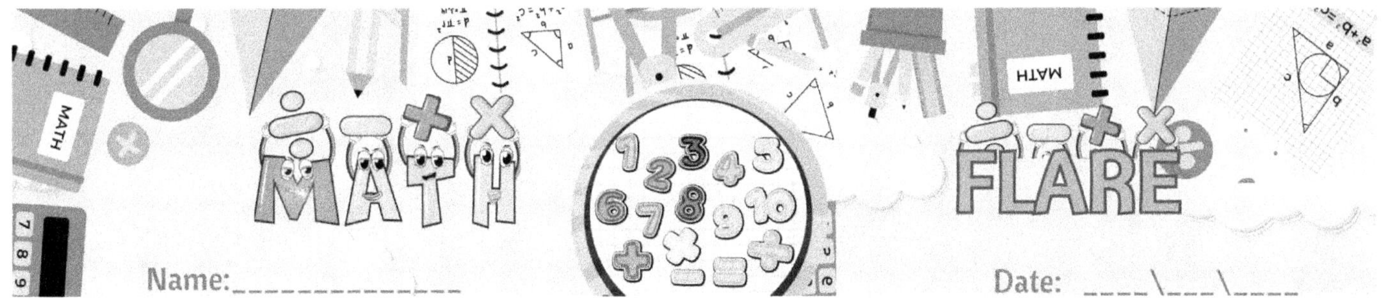

19. $3x + 3y = 1$

    $7x + 6y = 9$

20. $10x + 2y = 9$

    $3x + 2y = 2$

21. $4x + 3y = 7$

    $5x + 4y = 8$

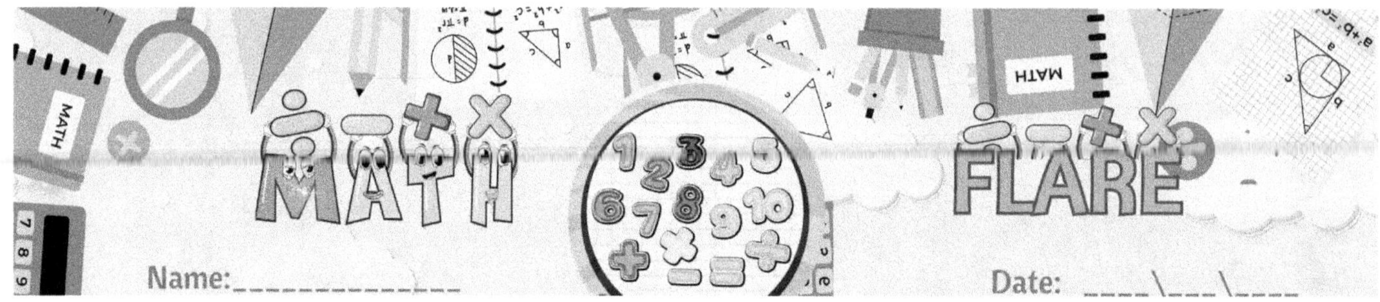

22. $6x + 7y = 10$

$6x + 1y = 3$

23. $4x + 1y = 9$

$7x + 9y = 1$

24. $10x + 7y = 1$

$5x + 8y = 8$

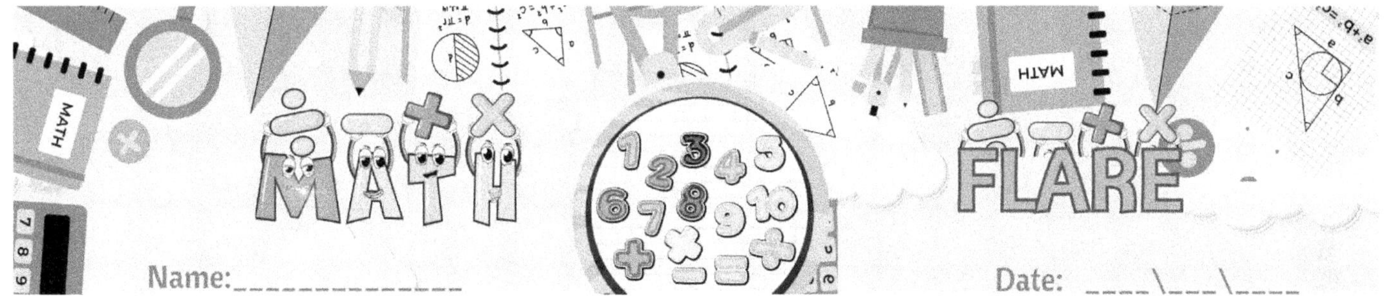

25. $10x + 5y = 4$

   $8x + 1y = 4$

26. $4x + 3y = 6$

   $6x + 3y = 9$

27. $5x + 9y = 6$

   $9x + 7y = 8$

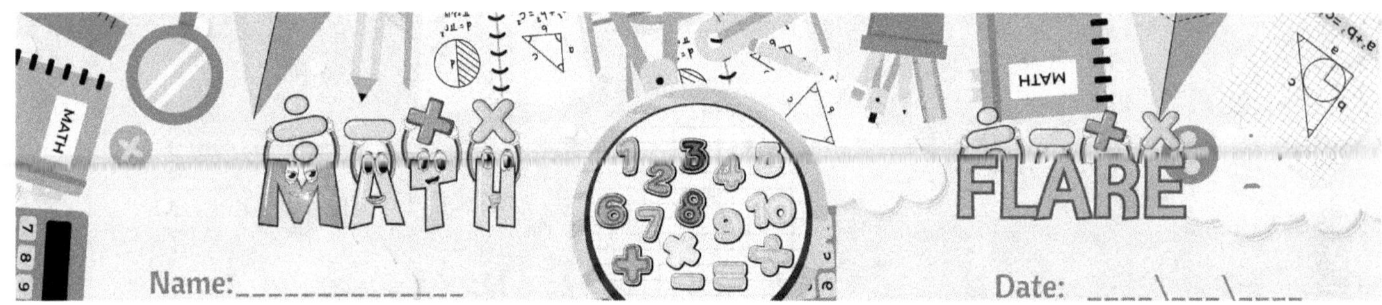

28. $10x + 8y = 10$

   $7x + 5y = 10$

29. $10x + 2y = 8$

   $6x + 10y = 7$

30. $7x + 5y = 2$

   $1x + 9y = 8$

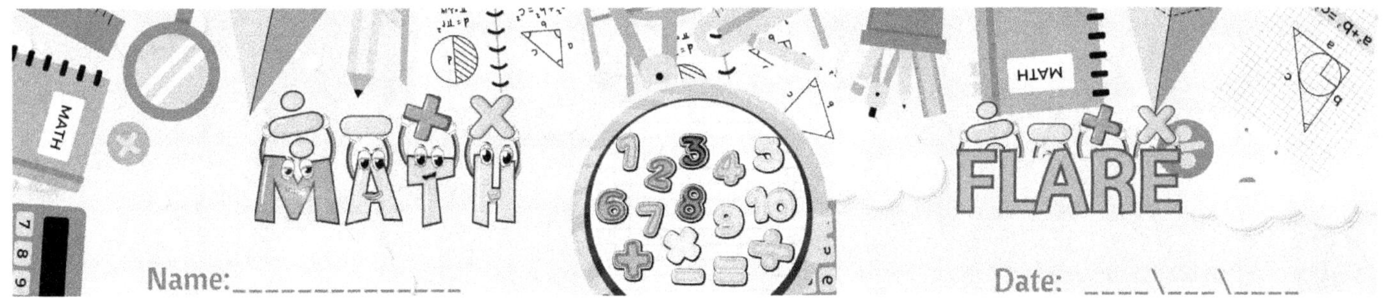

31. 3x + 5y = 1

    8x + 9y = 6

32. 9x + 8y = 7

    9x + 7y = 6

33. 9x + 8y = 7

    3x + 6y = 7

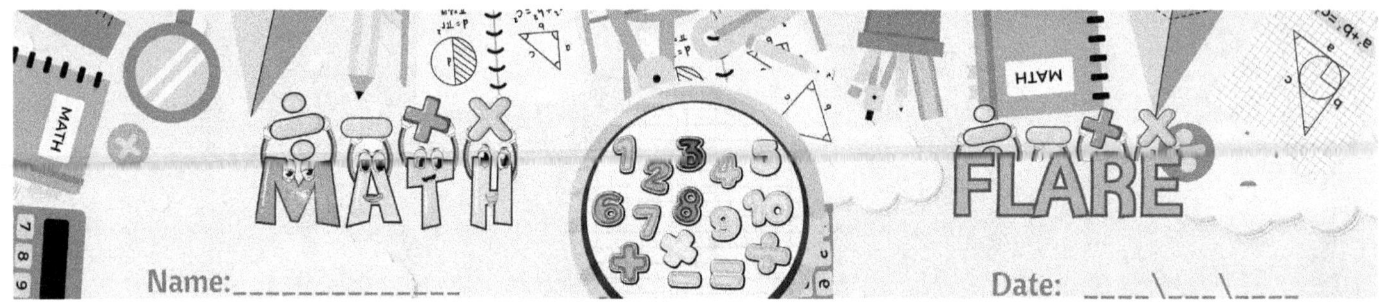

34. $5x + 1y = 3$

   $6x + 10y = 2$

35. $10x + 1y = 9$

   $6x + 7y = 4$

36. $2x + 7y = 8$

   $6x + 1y = 7$

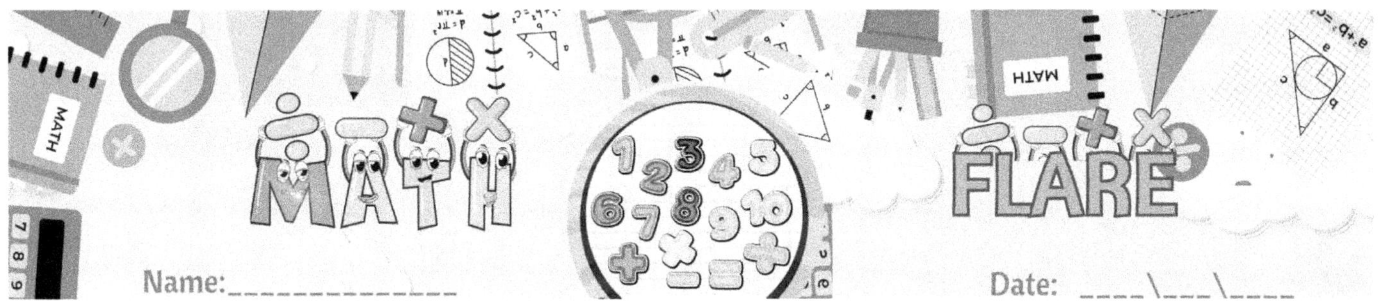

37. 7x + 10y = 7

2x + 5y = 3

38. 1x + 1y = 5

7x + 1y = 6

39. 2x + 1y = 7

5x + 5y = 3

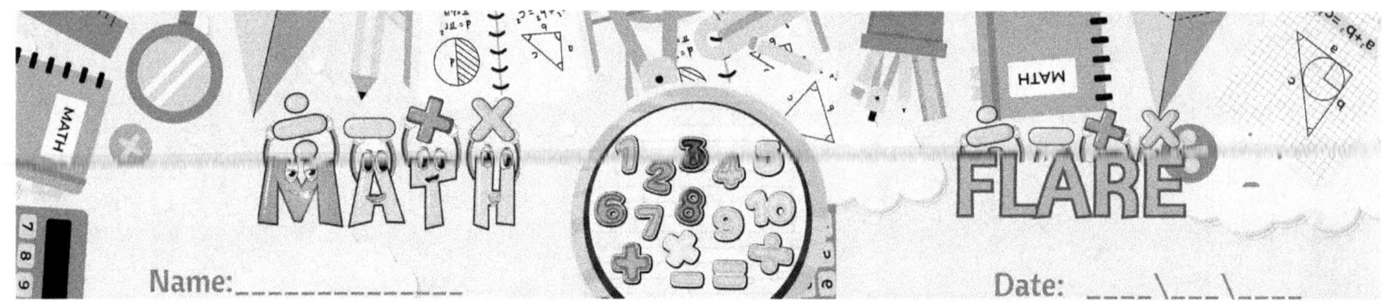

40. $4x + 3y = 5$

    $10x + 3y = 1$

41. $4x + 1y = 2$

    $2x + 9y = 7$

42. $6x + 4y = 4$

    $3x + 4y = 2$

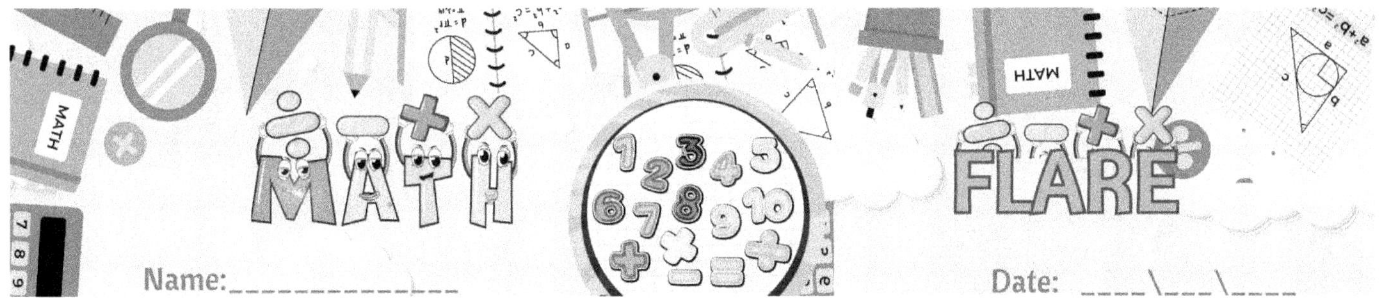

43. $4x + 4y = 2$

$4x + 7y = 10$

44. $6x + 7y = 7$

$3x + 2y = 9$

45. $3x + 8y = 2$

$2x + 3y = 2$

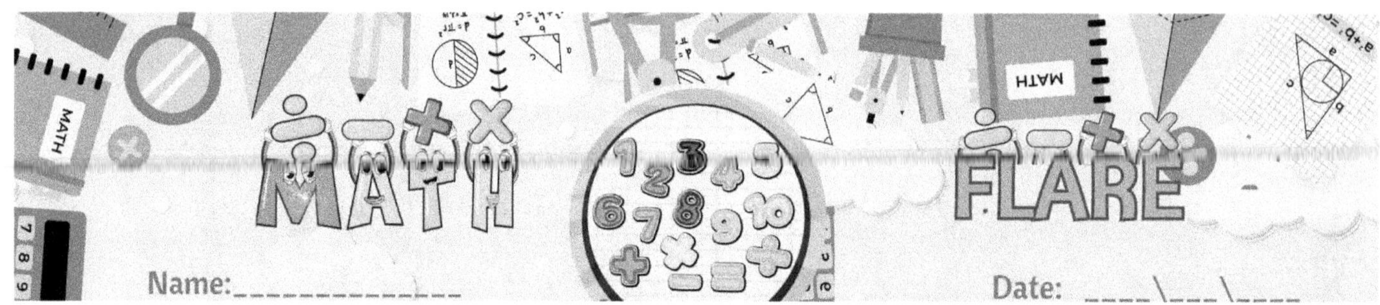

46. $1x + 9y = 9$

   $6x + 7y = 6$

47. $3x + 9y = 1$

   $2x + 10y = 2$

48. $2x + 6y = 5$

   $3x + 10y = 7$

49. $10x + 9y = 7$

$3x + 9y = 5$

50. $8x + 3y = 4$

$4x + 2y = 10$

ANSWERS

Page 1: Understanding Linear Functions

1. -23	21. 12	41. -11
2. -25	22. -20	42. 9
3. -18	23. 10	43. 6
4. -18	24. -38	44. -38
5. -46	25. 1	45. 12
6. 14	26. -5	46. 8
7. -9	27. 6	47. 1
8. 17	28. -10	48. 21
9. -10	29. 7	49. -1
10. -21	30. -11	50. 33
11. 4	31. -11	
12. -24	32. 15	
13. -47	33. 17	
14. -5	34. -8	
15. 10	35. 34	
16. 24	36. -31	
17. -3	37. 2	
18. 38	38. -6	
19. -29	39. 21	
20. 0	40. 1	

1. 3.0
2. -6.0
3. 9.0
4. -8.0
5. 8.0
6. -8.0
7. -4.0
8. 0.0
9. -1.0
10. -5.0
11. -8.0
12. 4.0
13. -3.0
14. 7.0
15. -9.0
16. 3.0
17. 6.0
18. -7.0
19. 6.0
20. 8.0
21. 3.0
22. -1.0
23. -4.0
24. -0.0
25. -10.0
26. -2.0
27. 1.0
28. 10.0
29. -4.0
30. 6.0
31. 6.0
32. 5.0
33. -8.0
34. 3.0
35. -7.0
36. 2.0
37. -6.0
38. -1.0
39. 0.0
40. 4.0
41. -0.0
42. -3.0
43. -7.0
44. -8.0
45. -2.0
46. -10.0
47. 7.0
48. -1.0
49. -6.0
50. -1.0
51. 1.0
52. 6.0
53. -3.0
54. 9.0
55. 6.0
56. -10.0
57. -4.0
58. 4.0
59. -6.0
60. 2.0
61. -4.0
62. -7.0
63. -10.0
64. -1.0
65. 4.0
66. -9.0
67. 5.0
68. 3.0
69. -4.0
70. 4.0
71. -2.0
72. -6.0
73. -7.0
74. -3.0
75. 8.0
76. 10.0
77. 4.0
78. 5.0
79. -5.0
80. -9.0
81. -2.0
82. -1.0
83. -10.0
84. -10.0
85. -9.0
86. 6.0
87. 7.0
88. -10.0
89. 3.0
90. 3.0
91. 8.0
92. -3.0
93. 4.0
94. 5.0
95. -2.0
96. -8.0

Page 16: Find Slope from Two Points

1. 7	21. -6	41. 4
2. 0	22. 7	42. 5
3. 10	23. 1	43. -5
4. 1	24. 10	44. 9
5. -7	25. 3	45. 4
6. 9	26. 2	46. -10
7. -4	27. 9	47. 1
8. 2	28. 8	48. -3
9. -10	29. 2	49. -2
10. 7	30. 9	50. -4
11. 5	31. -4	
12. 0	32. -9	
13. -3	33. -9	
14. -3	34. 5	
15. -10	35. -10	
16. -5	36. 4	
17. -5	37. 6	
18. 3	38. -6	
19. -7	39. -5	
20. -10	40. -7	

1.

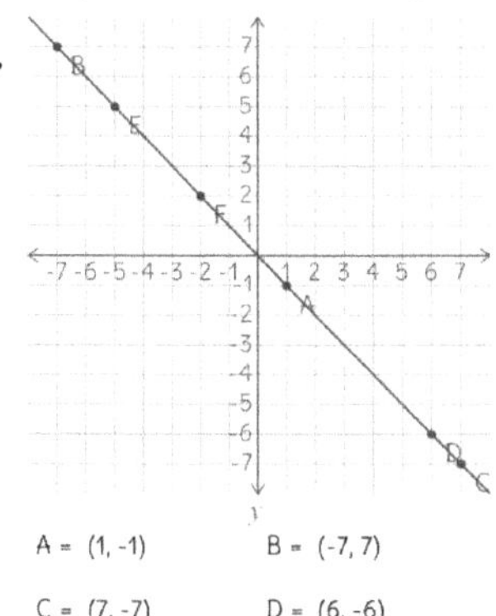

A = (1, -1)   B = (-7, 7)

C = (7, -7)   D = (6, -6)

E = (-5, 5)   F = (-2, 2)

2.

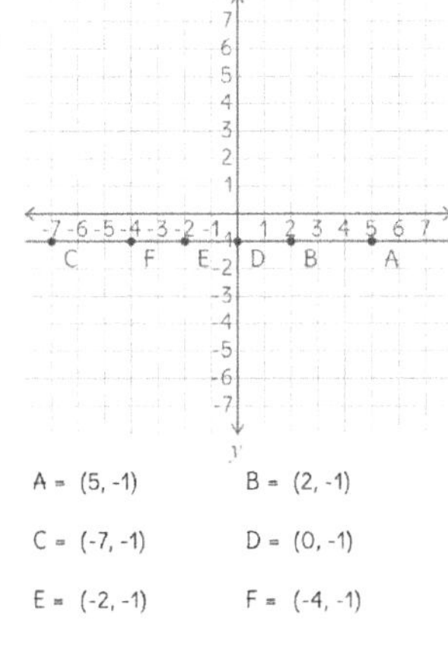

A = (5, -1)   B = (2, -1)

C = (-7, -1)   D = (0, -1)

E = (-2, -1)   F = (-4, -1)

3.

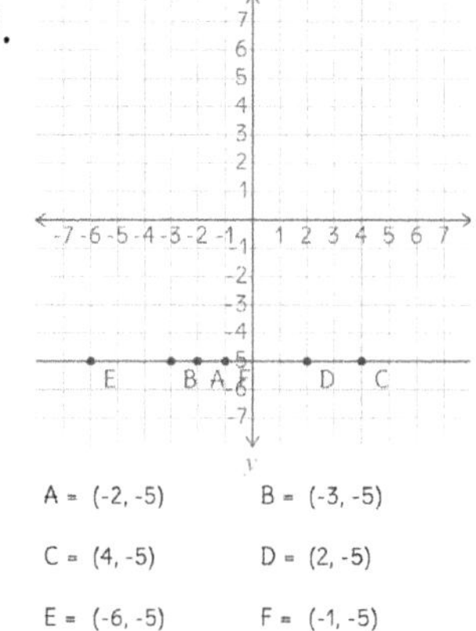

A = (-2, -5)   B = (-3, -5)

C = (4, -5)   D = (2, -5)

E = (-6, -5)   F = (-1, -5)

4.

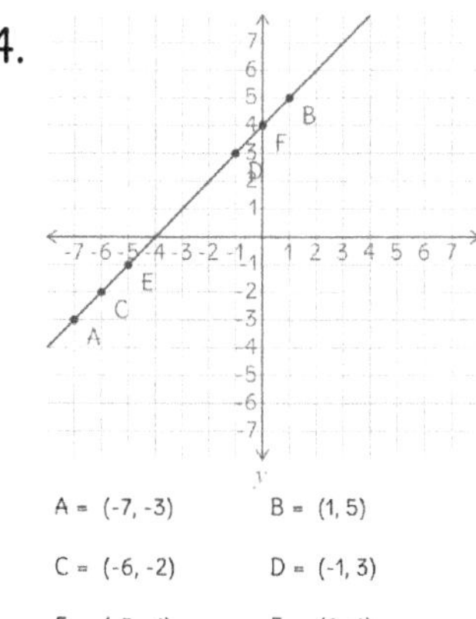

A = (-7, -3)   B = (1, 5)

C = (-6, -2)   D = (-1, 3)

E = (-5, -1)   F = (0, 4)

5.

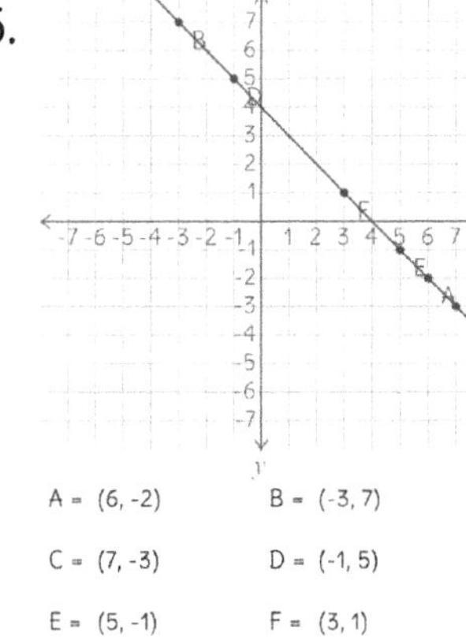

A = (6, -2)   B = (-3, 7)

C = (7, -3)   D = (-1, 5)

E = (5, -1)   F = (3, 1)

6.

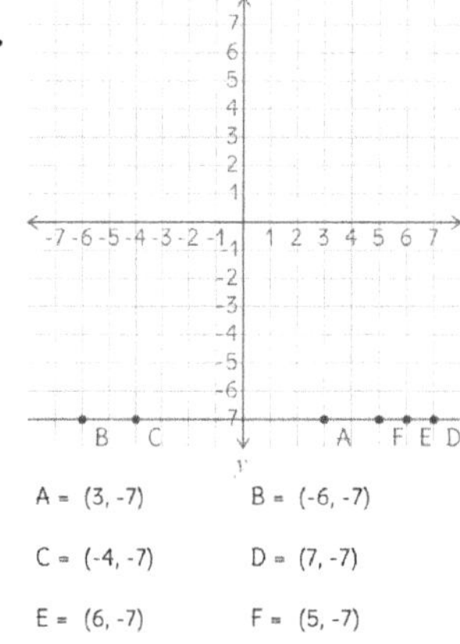

A = (3, -7)   B = (-6, -7)

C = (-4, -7)   D = (7, -7)

E = (6, -7)   F = (5, -7)

7. 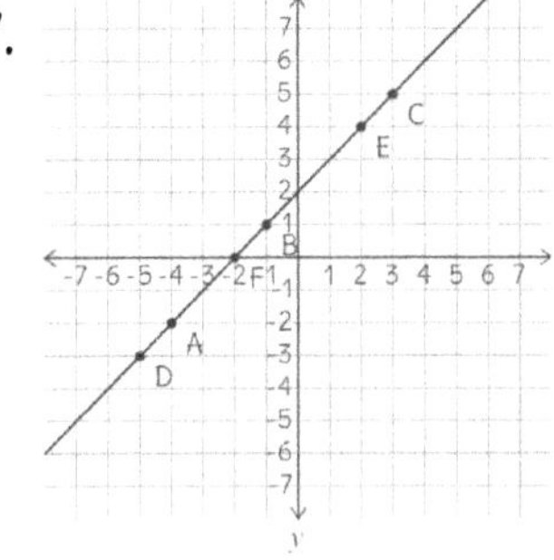

A = (-4, -2)   B = (-1, 1)

C = (3, 5)   D = (-5, -3)

E = (2, 4)   F = (-2, 0)

8. 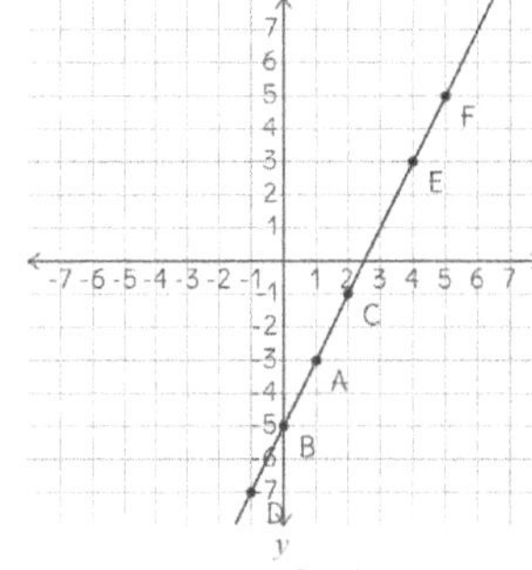

A = (1, -3)   B = (0, -5)

C = (2, -1)   D = (-1, -7)

E = (4, 3)   F = (5, 5)

9. 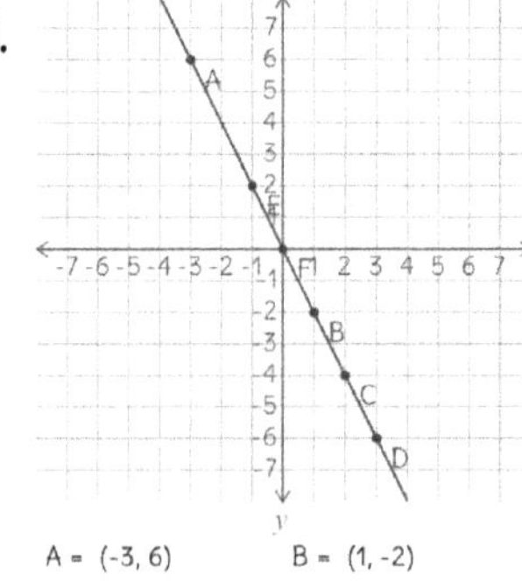

A = (-3, 6)   B = (1, -2)

C = (2, -4)   D = (3, -6)

E = (-1, 2)   F = (0, 0)

10. 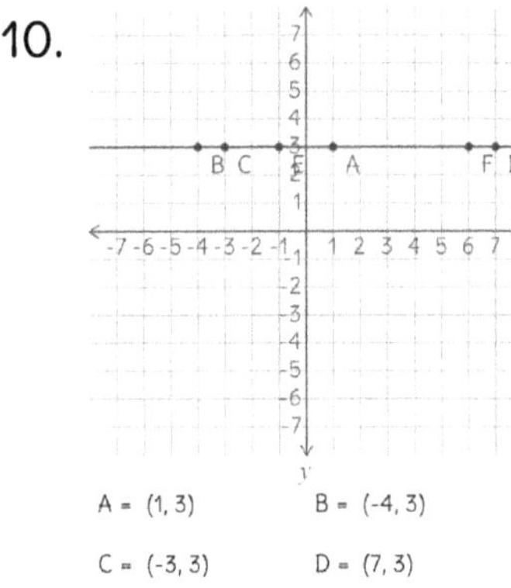

A = (1, 3)   B = (-4, 3)

C = (-3, 3)   D = (7, 3)

E = (-1, 3)   F = (6, 3)

Page 31: Graphing Linear Equations

1. $y = \frac{-1}{2}x + 6$

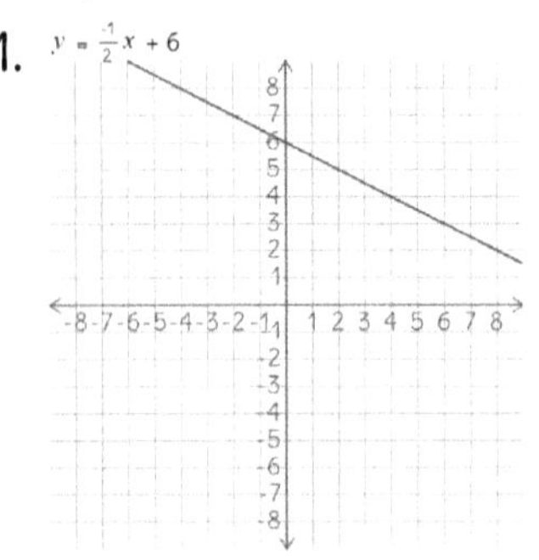

2. $y = \frac{3}{4}x$

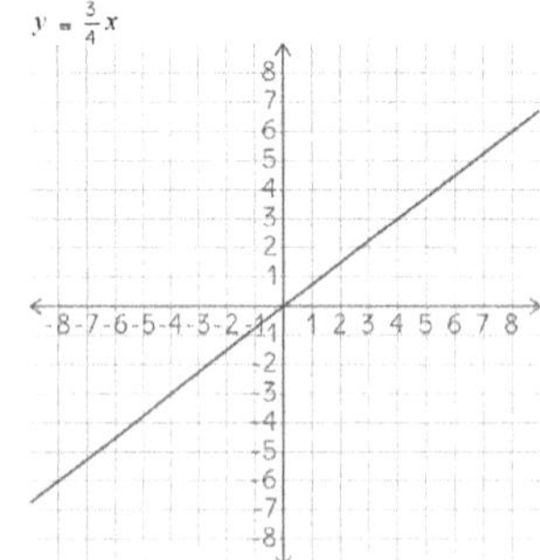

3. $x = 6$

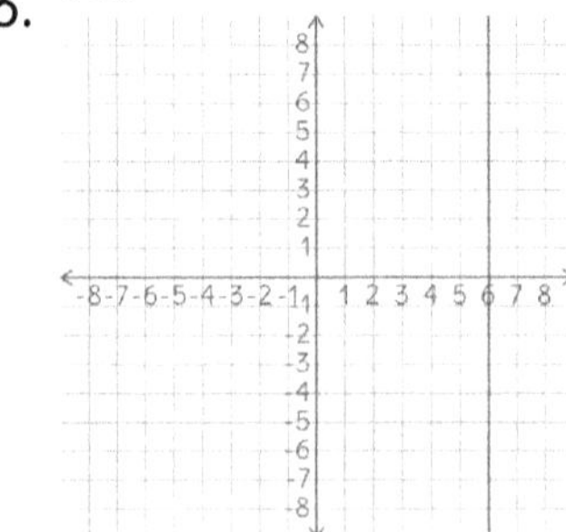

4. $y = \frac{-11}{4}x + 3$

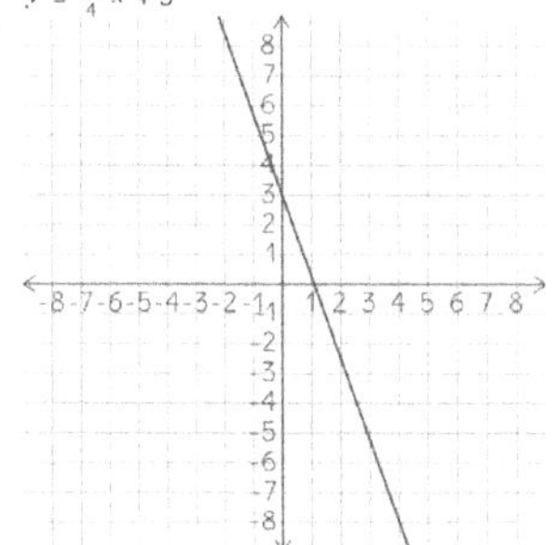

5. $y = x - 5$

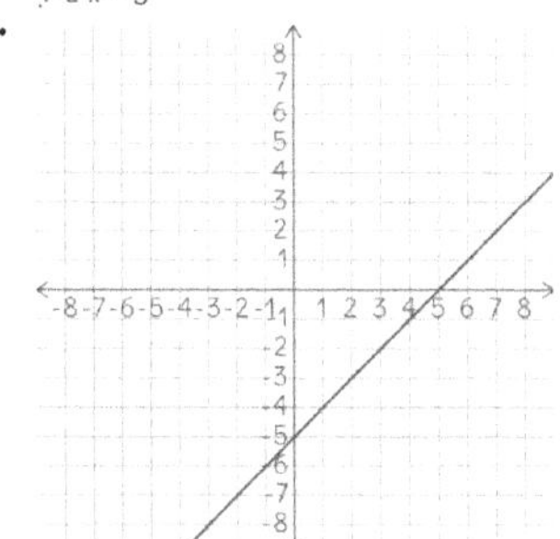

6. $y = -2x + 5$

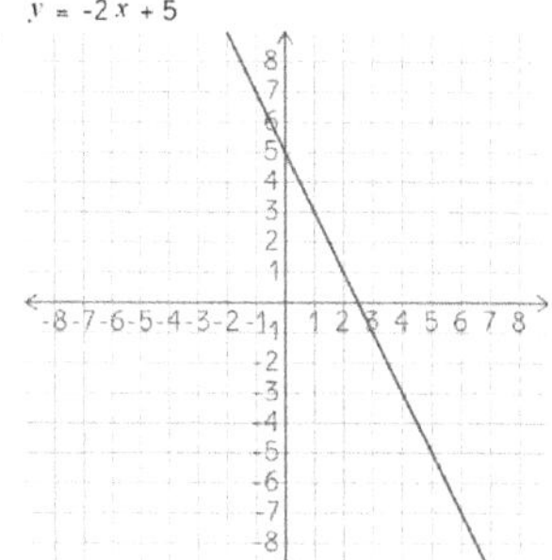

7. $y = \frac{-11}{4}x - 4$

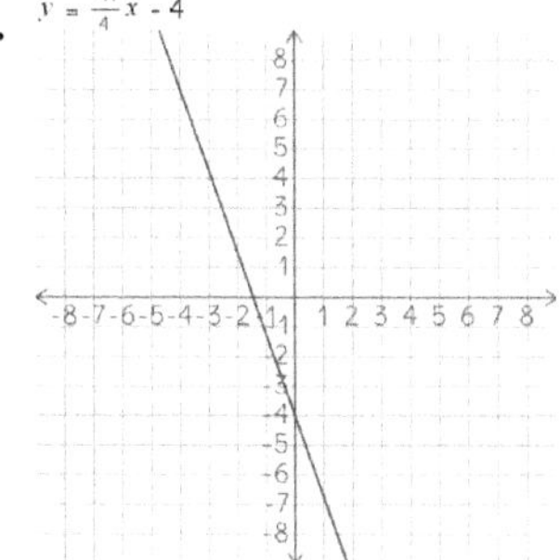

8. $y = -2x + 2$

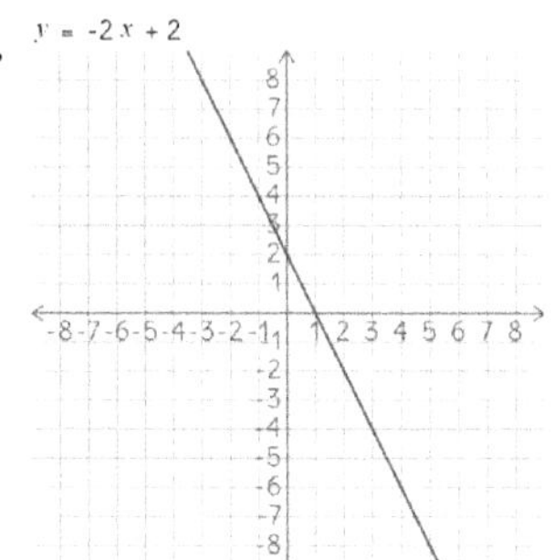

9. $y = \frac{1}{2}x - 8$

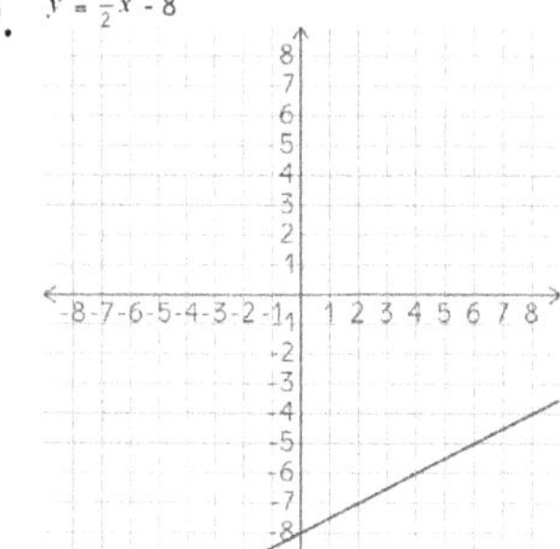

10. $y = 2x + 7$

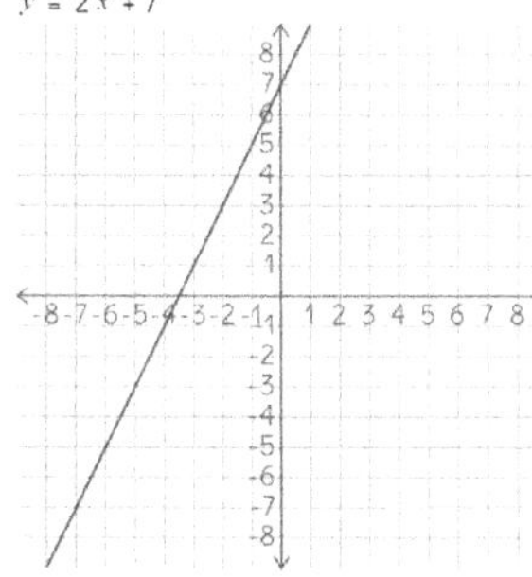

11. $y = \frac{-11}{4}x + 8$

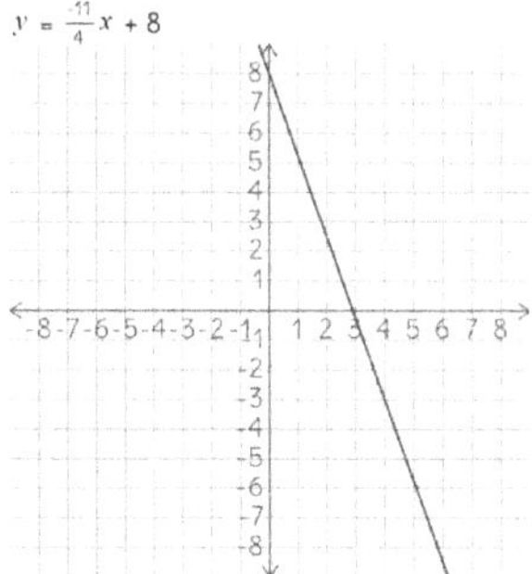

12. $y = \frac{-9}{4}x + 7$

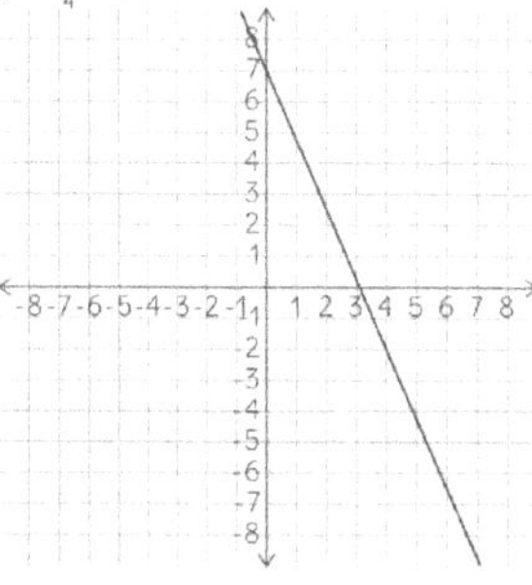

13. $y = \frac{1}{4}x + 3$

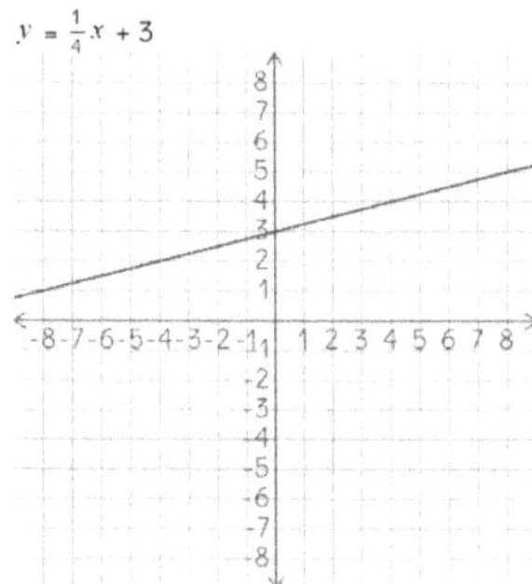

14. $y = \frac{-1}{2}x + 7$

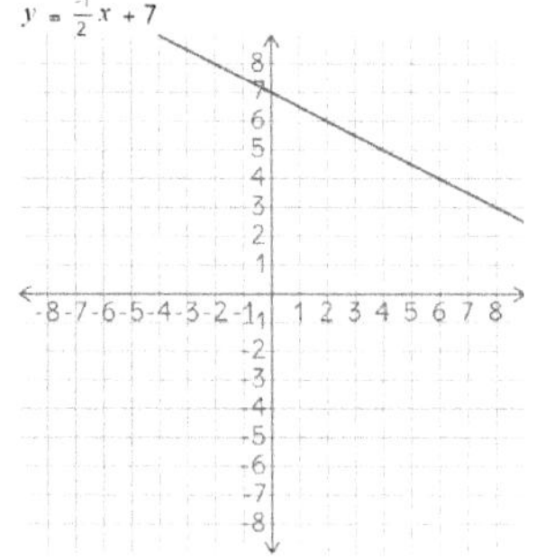

15. $y = \frac{7}{4}x + 8$

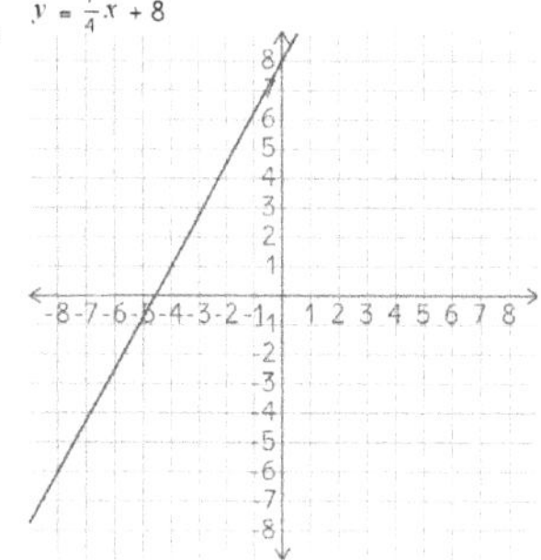

16. $y = \frac{3}{4}x - 1$

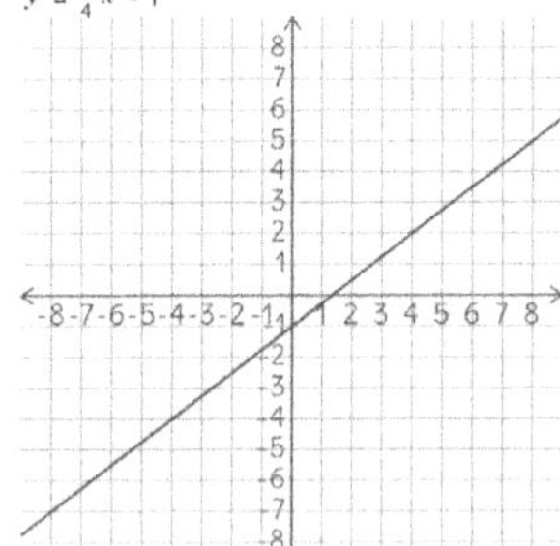

17. $y = \frac{3}{2}x + 3$

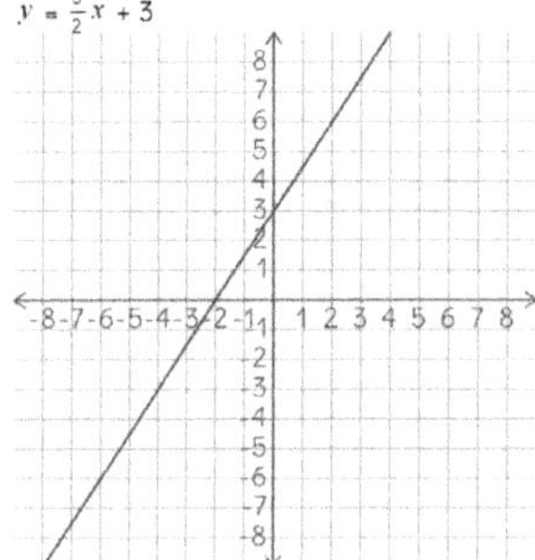

18. $y = \frac{11}{4}x - 1$

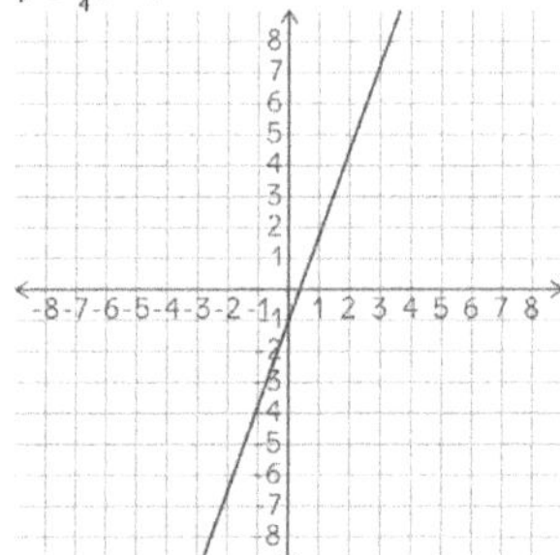

19. $y = -2x + 1$

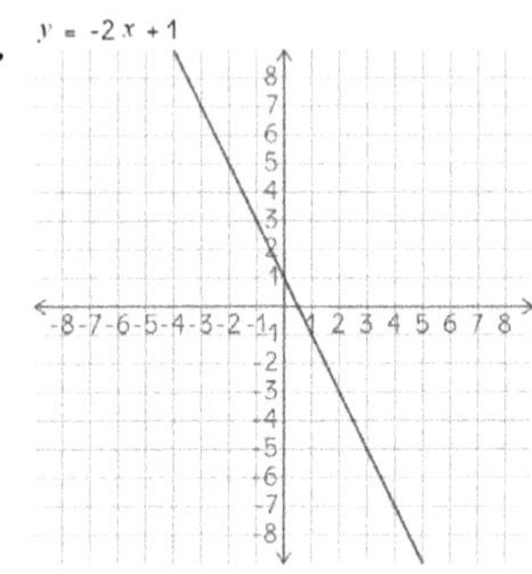

20. $y = -3x - 3$

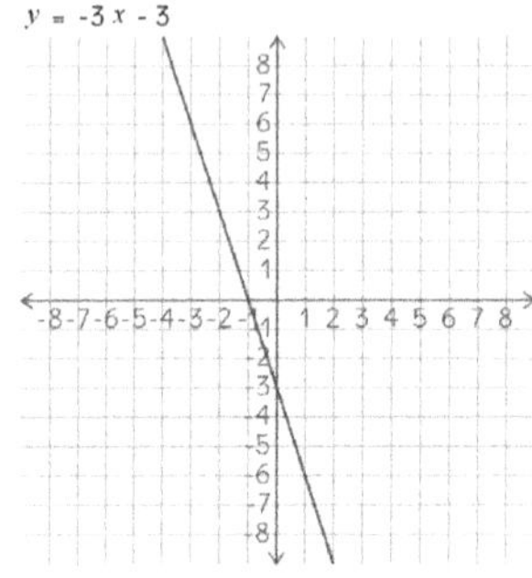

Page 51: System of Equations

1. x = 1.27, y = -0.09

2. x = 0.19, y = 0.09

3. x = 2.5, y = -4.75

4. x = -1.53, y = 1.63

5. x = -1.2, y = 4.2

6. x = 1.0, y = -0.8

7. x = -10.0, y = 24.0

8. x = 0.67, y = 0.22

9. x = 1.5, y = -0.0

10. x = -1.0, y = 0.5

11. x = -14.0, y = 6.5

12. x = -3.0, y = 3.0

13. x = 0.67, y = 4.33

14. x = -0.55, y = 1.73

15. x = 1.5, y = 0.0

16. x = 1.21, y = -0.05

17. x = 1.0, y = -0.0

18. x = 0.59, y = -0.31

19. x = 7.0, y = -6.67

20. x = 1.0, y = -0.5

21. x = 4.0, y = -3.0

22. x = 0.31, y = 1.17

23. x = 2.76, y = -2.03

24. x = -1.07, y = 1.67

25. x = 0.53, y = -0.27

26. x = 1.5, y = -0.0

27. x = 0.65, y = 0.3

28. x = 5.0, y = -5.0

29. x = 0.75, y = 0.25

30. x = -0.38, y = 0.93

31. x = 1.62, y = -0.77

32. x = -0.11, y = 1.0

33. x = -0.47, y = 1.4

34. x = 0.64, y = -0.18

35. x = 0.92, y = -0.22

36. x = 1.02, y = 0.85

37. x = 0.33, y = 0.47

38. x = 0.17, y = 4.83

39. x = 6.4, y = -5.8

40. x = -0.67, y = 2.56

41. x = 0.32, y = 0.71

42. x = 0.67, y = 0.0

43. x = -2.17, y = 2.67

44. x = 5.44, y = -3.67

45. x = 1.43, y = -0.29

46. x = -0.19, y = 1.02

47. x = -0.67, y = 0.33

48. x = 4.0, y = -0.5

49. x = 0.29, y = 0.46

50. x = -5.5, y = 16.0